THE
Empath's Quest
FINDING YOUR DESTINY

Bety Comerford and Steve Wilson

Author Photograph by Amanda Sullivan
Illustrations by Grace Anne Currier

Schiffer Publishing Ltd ®

4880 Lower Valley Road • Atglen, PA 19310

Library of Congress Control Number: 2016952636

Designed by Danielle D. Farmer
Cover design by Brenda McCallum

Paintings by Grace Anne Currier

Type set in Affair/Minion Pro/NewBskvll BT

ISBN: 978-0-7643-5223-2
Printed in China

Published by Schiffer Publishing, Ltd.
4880 Lower Valley Road
Atglen, PA 19310
Phone: (610) 593-1777; Fax: (610) 593-2002
E-mail: Info@schifferbooks.com
Web: www.schifferbooks.com

For our complete selection of fine books on this and related subjects, please visit our website at www.schifferbooks.com. You may also write for a free catalog.

Schiffer Publishing's titles are available at special discounts for bulk purchases for sales promotions or premiums. Special editions, including personalized covers, corporate imprints, and excerpts, can be created in large quantities for special needs. For more information, contact the publisher.

We are always looking for people to write books on new and related subjects. If you have an idea for a book, please contact us at proposals@schifferbooks.com.

Other Schiffer Books by the Author:
The Reluctant Empath. ISBN: 978-0-7643-4603-3

Other Schiffer Books on Related Subjects:
Paranormal Canadian Tales: A Supernatural Journey. Dawn Hunter Clark. ISBN: 978-0-7643-5207-2

The Psychic Workbook: Tools and Techniques to Develop Reliable Insight. Karen Fox, PhD. ISBN: 978-0-7643-4816-7

Develop Your Psychic Skills. Enid Hoffman. ISBN:914918-29-5

The Art of Mediumship: Psychic Investigation, Clairvoyance, and Channeling. Elaine Kuzmeskus. ISBN: 978-0-7643-4016-1

In Memory of...

Barbara, Carmen, Chris, Linda, Patty, and Teresa
Who believed...

To Otis, Missy, and Willow
Who loved unconditionally . . .

*When he shall die, cut him into little stars,
and he shall make the face of heaven so fond,
that all the world will fall in love with night and
pay no worship to the garish sun*

Contents

Introduction

THROUGHOUT HISTORY, there have been countless stories of heroes and heroines setting out on a quest. The 12 Labors of Hercules, the saga of Ulysses, the famous quest for the Holy Grail are only a few that come to mind. On each of these quests, the seekers had to go through many trials and tribulations to reach what they sought. Along the way, they ended up learning more about themselves than about the task at hand. When they finally accomplished their quest, when they had overcome all the lessons their quest set out for them, they were rewarded with a love so deep and abiding, there are no words to describe it.

Is this same need, this same quest to reach an understanding of our lives within all of us? As empathic people, we're always having energetic experiences—many times whether we want to or not. In fact, we believe everyone has these experiences whether they're empathic or not. Yet, the end result is that rather than taking a step back and trying to learn what each of these energetic experiences is trying to teach us, we instead try to shut down, or protect ourselves, from what we're feeling. As we tell our students, you have to do whatever you need to do to make yourself feel comfortable. However, here is another thought we'd like you to consider.

When you shut down or protect yourself from the energies you feel, are you shutting down or protecting yourself against learning an important lesson that will help you realize what your empathy and your life means? Are you turning away from your quest to experience energy in its purest form—that love that no words can possibly describe?

We are the first to say—bad things happen. But as an empath, you have the ability to get to that place where you realize there's more to the story. There is a lesson to be learned. And it is this lesson that drives us on our quest to know more—to get to that space where bad things can turn into good things. We'd like to share an example of what we're talking about.

Several years ago, Steve was counseling a woman who'd been diagnosed with terminal cancer. It's understandable that anyone who is given such a diagnosis is going to go into an emotional tailspin. The doctors said she had six months to live. She ended up living two years. At the end of those two years, she told Steve that she realized the cancer was the most wonderful thing to happen to her. When Steve asked her what she meant by that, she explained, "It gave me a relationship with God." Now, you may not believe in a Supreme Being. But this woman felt love in the purest sense from a source outside herself. She'd come to a place within herself where she'd made peace with her life and how it was going to end. She turned a bad thing into a good thing. When she died, she died in a state of serene grace and love.

Many people manifest their reality based on their past experiences. They're constantly bringing their past into their present and future. They shine their light on a movie they've created of their life. They watch and live that movie over and over again, not changing it, turning away from the possibility that the movie can be modified and edited. Because of fears that are based on past experiences, they turn away from the drive we all have to feel higher amounts of that perfect love we all seek. Many feel that perfect love in nature. Why can't we feel it in human interaction?

Is our life just a set of crazy happenstance? Do we really have any control over our lives? As empaths, do we really need to spend the rest of our days feeling the crappy energy from everyone around us? From the world itself?

If you've read our previous books, *Ghosts and Shamanic Tales of True Hauntings* and *The Reluctant Empath*, you'll know our basic philosophy is that everything is made up of energy. You, your pets, the trees in your yard, the rocks in the woods, the flowers in your planter, the wild animals—all are made up of energy. And, as energy, it has a particular vibration to it. If your personal vibration is high, you feel good, healthy, at peace. You're better able to handle the trials and tribulations you will find on your quest to understanding who you are. If your personal vibration is low, you feel heavy, depressed, sad, or angry, remaining stuck in what seems an interminable treadmill of a life not fulfilled.

Many of you may have heard the term "sacred geometry." We've come to understand that these geometric figures that reside in your energy field hold the lessons you've come to this life to learn. Some will be easy. Some will not be so easy. But with each lesson learned, you are released from its hold and you are able to move along to the next lesson.

Comprehending how this all works allows you to understand why "bad" things happen and why "good" things happen. It allows you to make peace with the process because you know there is a plan to each of our lives. There is a reason behind the madness we call life.

Underpinning all this is the human desire for love. It is love that propels us forward in everything: Love of comfort, love of money, love of another person. Many times this love isn't love at all. It's control.

How do we move past that?

There's a method, a plan, a synchronicity to the universe that all falls into place when one understands how the plan works. There is something called the timeline, which will be explored in depth in the following pages. Every living creature on this planet has a timeline. And upon this timeline is the geometry of the lessons that, once learned, propel us further along that timeline. Understanding the timeline will help you comprehend why your life is the way it is.

Our decision to write this book lies in seeing so many people stumble through their life, not understanding why they experience what they experience, why they can't attain what they want, or if they do attain what they think will make them happy, discover that they're still not satisfied. They keep striving for what they think will fulfill them, but it's not enough. It's never enough.

This book will teach you how to reach that point when it *is* enough.

We wrote this to help whoever picks up this book to comprehend how much they can contribute to the unfoldment of their own destiny. It isn't haphazard. It isn't left to blow in the wind. You can choose to embrace your path and see where it takes you.

Understanding the love and energy behind your destiny, acquainting yourself with your own personal timeline, releasing the geometry that moves you forward on that timeline, and knowing how it all works together will assist you to make better choices, to overcome the difficulties in life we all experience, and live the life you were meant to live.

In order to take such a complex subject and present it in a comprehensive, logical way, we've decided to use Alex again. Introduced in *The Reluctant Empath*, Alex will be your stand-in. This time, he is joined by three women of differing experiences with spirituality and energy. What they experience, what they learn, and how they deal with situations will be your road map to how you deal with similar circumstances. We will take it step by step as your destiny and your empathic quest unfolds. If you've been following Alex throughout *The Reluctant Empath*, you may find a few topics familiar in this book, such as manifestation and intention. Here, we will be delving deeper, building upon and expanding those subjects to give you a richer understanding of the possibilities you have at your disposal to create a happier life for yourself.

There will be theories here that may poke at you, upset you, even make you angry. We ask that you bear with us as you continue to read. There's a reason why we are writing what we are writing.

Once again, everything that is described in this book has happened to one or both of us. Nothing is made up. The realizations, the lessons, the situations are those we have lived through in our own personal journeys.

Know that the story you are about to read isn't just a collection of anecdotes. It is a life. Steve's life. My life. Your life. It's that simple; it's that humble.

Prologue

THE ENGINES KICKED ON, sending a low hum throughout the plane. A moment later, there was a lurch, followed by the ever so slow movement as the jet backed away from the gate.

Alex's heart beat with each turn of the plane's wheels while his hands unconsciously gripped the armrests. It wasn't that he was afraid—well, that wasn't exactly true. He *was* a little nervous. He'd had enough visions of past lives killed in plane crashes not to be a little apprehensive every time he flew. Yet what stoked his apprehension was the weight of feeling the anxiety of almost every passenger on the sold-out flight. He'd long ago discovered he was an empath—a human sponge who soaked up every emotion and thought and feeling from those around him. Because of his empathy, he'd had to learn how to cope with all the different energies that constantly bombarded him. He'd had no choice, really. The alternative would have been to hide away in his closet for the rest of his life. Not a very viable option.

One of his most valuable lessons was learning how to hold his own space and not allow those energies to overwhelm him. With nearly a hundred people on this flight, he felt a potent mixture of their fears, their anxiety, their restlessness, and their anticipation.

He didn't allow himself to add his own emotions to the jumble, knowing that would compound the heaviness around him and within him. Instead, he began to ground out what he was feeling—allowing it to move, unimpeded, through him. In no time at all, the passengers' anxieties he'd felt in his chest and stomach melted away and he now felt his own excitement grow as the plane started its lumbering journey away from the terminal.

He glanced around him, seeing the faces scattered throughout the cabin of the three women he was traveling with. Cora and Keri were new to the world of spirituality and energy, joining Alex's small group of students within the last year. Zoey was a former student and now a cherished friend, who'd experienced many of the deep healings and energetic experiences walking her spiritual path presented. She'd come a long way in the fifteen years since first meeting Alex. She understood many of the deeper teachings and Alex knew that when he shared his crazy experiences with her, she was one of the few who completely understood, since she'd lived through most of them herself.

Each member of his little group looked and felt as eager as he did. He wasn't surprised. This trip was more than just a check on their imaginary bucket list. After scrimping and saving for months, they were on the first leg of a journey that would change their lives in ways no one could predict.

They were on their way to Arizona.

He couldn't quite remember how this trip had even come up in the first place. Yet, once it was spoken of, he knew he had to go. They'd each had a pull to go on this trip. Why remained to be seen.

Whatever the reasons, Alex knew it would change their lives in ways none of them could begin to imagine. They just needed to keep an open heart and an open mind to whatever adventures awaited them.

It was both exhilarating and frightening.

Alex laid his head back and closed his eyes. Mingled with his eagerness and joy was a deep sense of awe. At fifty years old, he'd been through what sometimes felt like three lifetimes rolled into one. His spiritual experiences had taken him into deep journeys, not only within himself but into the world and universe around him. They'd provided him with the desire to share all he'd learned with others by becoming a spiritual teacher. He smiled as he asked himself the question he never tired of asking. How did I ever get to this point in my life?

How was it that he'd experienced so many highs, so many lows, so many deeply felt spiritual adventures? What was it about him that allowed him to courageously take those steps into a deeper understanding of why he was created, why he walked the particular path he was on, why the Universe had provided him with, after so many years of going it alone, a wonderful group of friends who were more than friends? They were his spiritual family who were now on this plane, awaiting their own personal voyages in a land awash with spirituality and community with what the Hopi civilization called the Star Elders.

Alex grinned as he pondered all these things.

The plane turned. The engines roared. With a burst of speed, it hurtled down the runway until, as smoothly as ice skaters gliding across a frozen pond, it lifted up. And up. Into a bank of clouds, followed by a view of the bluest sky he'd ever seen.

They were on their way. Just as he'd been led every step of the way in his life's journey. What once appeared to be coincidence, Alex now knew was meant to happen. Each one of his traveling companions had intersected his life at just the right moment, seeking what he was seeking. Longing to understand their spiritual gifts, their place in the world, why they'd been created.

Just as he had.

Settling back in his chair, Alex cast his mind back, marveling at how all the strings that made up his life somehow worked together to get him to this point in time.

Recalling the lessons that ultimately served to get him to his destiny, he remembered many of the energetic choices he'd had to make to move his vibration that much closer to knowing what he considered God. He'd learned there was no good or bad, just options along the way that brought him up, one rung at a time, to understanding the universe and where he fit into its Grand Plan. Before he knew it, he was no longer on the plane, but lost in memories of years before when he'd first placed his footprint on a journey that he never could or would have imagined…

The Nature of Reality

ALEX GREW UP A CURIOUS CHILD. He was forever poking and prodding, asking questions about subjects the adults around him had no interest in or answers for. Born into a world before the Internet made its debut, Alex spent countless hours at his local library, lovingly running his fingers along the bindings of books that he knew would gain him a deeper understanding of whatever had initially piqued his interest. Already feeling too much of the emotions of those around him, he craved the silence and serenity of the library where the only emotions he felt were his own as he embarked on endless treks through the pages of books. He became a fixture at the research table, so much so that the librarians took to keeping his chair reserved until he showed up punctually at 3:15 to begin his mental voyages into a vast world he could only gain access to, at such a young age, through the written word.

When he was fourteen years old, he watched a program on television that spoke of the Garden of Eden. The concept of good and evil, all encompassed in a seemingly innocent looking apple used to tempt Eve, intrigued him. He pondered it for days, never quite grasping what it was he was looking for, or why the subject of the apple wouldn't quite leave him alone.

About a week later, Alex went to bed munching on, of all things, an apple. Leaving the half-eaten fruit on his bedside table, he fell asleep.

And dreamed of the apple.

In the vividness of his dream, Alex found himself standing in front of a tall, imposing black wall. Challenged by the starkness of the wall, he jumped up and down, trying to see over, but it was too high. He tried going around, but looking to his right, then his left, all he saw stretching on indefinitely was the black wall.

An uneasy feeling started to come over him as he realized he was trapped. *Where am I?* he thought frantically to himself as panic started to set in. *Why am I here?*

He turned away from the wall and stopped short, his heart racing in fear. It was as though he'd stepped off a page in a book and was enveloped in a void of white. Everywhere he looked, all he saw was white. Except for the large, black wall.

The emptiness frightened him even more.

Suddenly the hairs on the back of his neck stood up and a tingling rushed through his body.

He was being watched.

With his throat dry and his heart pounding in his chest, Alex slowly turned back around to face the wall. His eyes traveled upwards and he caught his breath.

On the top of the wall, with his legs dangling over the edge, sat a man dressed in a white robe. A glow of luminescent light sparkled about him. His round face beamed with a peaceful smile and his eyes were the bluest Alex had ever seen.

"Hello, Alex," he greeted, his voice low and pleasing to the ear.

Alex stared at the figure. He looked somewhat familiar, but he couldn't quite place him. Before he could stop himself, he blurted out, "Who are you?"

"My name isn't important at the moment. What is important is your quest to comprehend how the apple fits into the Garden of Eden and your quest for love. There have been moments when you have felt a love so profound there are no words for it, correct?"

Alex thought back to those times he'd be in the woods, sitting with his back up against a tree, watching the animals go about their business, when suddenly he would be filled up with a love so deep that seemed to come out of nowhere. It was so intense, it would almost make him cry.

"That's true," he admitted.

"Now, think about those situations where you've heard humans tell you or others they love them, yet somehow, you have felt the falsity of their words. It's as if you could physically feel that what they were saying wasn't true." Alex nodded. "In those moments when you have felt love from people, you've still known deep inside yourself, there's something missing. There must be more."

Alex was dumbfounded. And intrigued. So far what this strange man was saying was incredibly accurate. If he could really help Alex find this love that he so richly knew was to be had, whether in his own little world or outside somewhere, he was ready to listen and understand. He sat down cross-legged on the ground and looked up at the man.

"Please. I'd really like to learn about love and why I'm here. And this Garden thing . . . for some reason, reading about it made me mad."

"Rightfully so. So many people are angry about the Garden in one way or another. Even if they don't quite believe in the actual existence of the Garden of Eden, they still are seeking to return to what they had there."

"Which was?"

The old man smiled. "They had perfection. They had a love so deep and so satisfying, words cannot describe it."

Alex pondered this for a moment. "If this Garden really did exist and we had those things, why did we ever leave it?"

The man nodded. "Excellent question. How would you feel if you were given everything you ever wanted, just like that, with a snap of the fingers?"

"Everything?" Alex asked.

"Everything."

"I think it would be cool!"

"At first. But what if this happened day in day out, year after year, decade after decade, millennia after millennia?"

"Mmmmm. I think I'd be bored."

The man chuckled. "Very good. So humans left the Garden because they were bored. Because they thought things would be better or more interesting on the other side. When they departed, they were given the greatest gift they could have received. They received the gift of free will. Unfortunately, they weren't given a manual on how to use this free will correctly. Instead, they became immersed in fear, fear of lack, fear of not being loved, fear of losing the perfection they'd once taken for granted. Humans have spent eons trying to find their back way to the perfection they walked away from. They learned to manifest what they thought would make them happy. But it hasn't quite worked, has it?"

Alex shook his head. "Nobody seems to know how to be really happy."

The man reached behind him and withdrew a large shiny apple in his palm. Holding it up for Alex to see, the boy marveled at its perfection. It was the largest and shiniest apple he'd ever seen. Its deep red color contrasted sharply with the blackness of the wall and the stark white of his surroundings. He watched as the man took a bite of the apple. He then held it up.

"What do you see in the middle of this apple?"

Alex peered at it. "It looks like a star."

"Exactly. Every apple has a star at its core. Do you know what the star represents?"

"Um, the seeds that created the apple?"

The man smiled. "That's right. But although these seeds are important, there's something else I want you to understand." He pointed to each side of the star. "Each corner of the star represents an element. This is the nature of reality, the energy of the earth."

Alex didn't quite understand what the man was trying to tell him. Seeing the confusion on the teenager's face, the stranger continued, "All things that are experienced upon the earth are manifested into a physical state from the elements. Do you know what I mean when I use the word elements?"

Alex shook his head. He'd never heard the term before.

"Everything on this planet is made up of the energies of earth, water, fire, and air. In the center is spirit. Every culture, no matter its location or how old it is, has a story or legend that explains the energy of this star and what it represents. I know you're still a bit young to fully understand what all this means, but I promise you that over the next few years, it will become clearer to you. You will see for yourself how different cultures work with the energy of the star." The man's smile broadened. "Your quest has begun, my boy."

And with that, the man disappeared and Alex awoke in his bed.

With his curiosity at fever pitch, Alex found himself obsessed with the concept of the four elements. He had to find out what they were all about. All that day he impatiently waited for school to end. When the bell stuck three, he rushed to the library and was soon lost behind a stack of books.

One of the first books he flipped through was one dedicated to Native American lore. Opening it up at random, he was astonished to see a picture of a medicine wheel. He grew excited as he realized its resemblance to the star in the center of the apple he'd been shown in his dream the night before.

He eagerly dove into the text and soon discovered that each corner of the medicine wheel represented a direction. The East was associated with the Element of Air. The South was fire. The West was Water. The North was Earth.

Reading further, he found that each direction had an animal that served as its guardian. Although there were no set rules as to what animal represented a particular direction, he noticed animals were used that were familiar to the specific culture.

For the North American native tribes, Buffalo represented the North, Mouse represented the South, the Eagle represented the East and the Bear represented the West. For the South American people, Hummingbird represented the North, Jaguar represented the West, East was Eagle and South was Snake.

Spurred on by his discovery, he delved into the other books, noticing that cultures as far apart as North and South America and the Far East shared the same concept of the elements, the directions and their animal guardians.

Even the Bible made a reference to the elements. When describing heaven, Revelations 4:7 mentioned four creatures standing around the throne of God, which Alex was able to equate to the four fixed signs of the zodiac. They were a figure of a lion, Leo, which represented the fire element; an ox, Taurus, which represented the earth element; the face of a man, Aquarius, which represented the air element; and Scorpio as the ancient symbol of the Eagle, which represented the water element.

He knew then he was on to something. He reached for the last book and found himself staring at a symbol known as a pentagram. It looked very much like the star in his dream. He knew many people believed the pentagram to be a symbol of evil. But he knew this wasn't so. It all came down to human intention. If humanity labeled something as bad, then it was seen as bad, especially when the labeling came from a place of misinformation or misinterpretation. Alex knew enough to look beyond the human label and feel the energy. Seeing the star shape within the pentagram and feeling its energy made him feel good inside.

Alex spent the next few days reading what he could about the elements and the lore surrounding the Garden of Eden. However, at fourteen years of age, other things gradually took his attention and this particular subject was put aside.

The years went by and Alex turned seventeen. He fell in with a group of new friends and was astonished when the subject of the mystical star and the elements that had so fascinated him three years before, came up again.

It turned out these new friends were captivated with druidism. As far as he was concerned, druidism had something to do with Merlin, King Arthur, and Camelot. Yet as Alex listened to their daily discussions, he was amazed to discover that druidism was much more. As they spoke of their affinity to nature and the belief of a connection of spirit in all things, it struck a chord in him. He'd always found solace in nature. The woods behind his house were his refuge and he spent hours there, his stress and anxiety pooling away, replaced by a sense of peace from the surrounding trees and flowers.

When they brought up the subject of the elements, Alex remembered his dream. He asked if they knew anything about the star.

"Oh yeah," answered Mike, who at eighteen, was the oldest of the group. "The star represents the energy of the earth." He grinned. "I bet you didn't know that you can use these energies to make things happen."

Throughout his readings, Alex had come across the concept of manifestation, but he hadn't quite understood what it meant. Perhaps his friend could provide the answer. "How does that work?" he asked.

"I was just reading about this the other night. Check it out. When you speak, where do your words go?"

"Into the air," Alex answered.

"Exactly." Mike pulled out a notebook and flipped through it until he found what he was looking for. "I took notes because it just blew my mind. Now listen." He began to read.

There is power and intention in the spoken word. You intend your words to be heard, to be acted upon. There is also power in the Element of Air itself which, as it takes your words, adds its own intention to hold your words once they have left your body. Adding fire, which is your passion, to your words, you are, in effect, giving your intention more fuel to unfold. The element of water now assists the energy of your words to flow to that place where it needs to go. Finally, the element of earth allows your words to become physical. If it's all done properly, then the Spirit of all things resides in the center. When this happens, you have yourself a fine manifestation.

Mike looked up, his eyes bright with excitement. "What do you think of that?"

Alex was mesmerized. It made so much sense. That night, sitting in his room, he recalled the initial dream that had put him on his quest to discover the meaning of the star. Someway, somehow, the star was integral in manifesting things into being.

But how?

He closed his eyes and concentrated. If I'm meant to find out the secret of the star and how it's involved in manifestation, please let me know in the dreamtime.

His prayer was answered.

Many years after the initial dream, he once again found himself in the dreamtime standing in front of the familiar black wall. However, there was a difference.

This time there was a door.

Trusting that whatever was on the other side was there to teach him, Alex gathered his courage.

Here goes nothing, he thought to himself as he stepped forward and walked through the door.

He was immediately struck by the vibrancy of the garden he found himself in. It was lush and awash with spectacular colors. Around him were birds and animals of all shapes and sizes, of deep turquoise feathers and luxurious, gleaming fur. None were afraid of him. Soothing rich perfume from surrounding flowers filled his nostrils. There was a peace and serenity here he'd never experienced before. Looking about, an astonishing idea began to form. Could it be? Was it possible?

Had Alex entered the Garden of Eden itself?

A path appeared in front of him and he began to follow it, plunging him deeper into this magical land.

Walking along, he realized he was hungry. He wondered if any of the trees around him had fruit he could eat. To his surprise, a banana suddenly popped up in front of him. Tentatively reaching out, he was amazed to see that it was real and tangible. Peeling it, he ate the banana.

Soon, things were popping up that he hadn't even visualized yet. It was as though someone or something was anticipating his needs and giving it to him before he realized he needed or wanted it.

Before he could fully grasp why this was happening, he abruptly found himself back on the other side of the wall. As quickly as he'd been in the place of perfection, he was now back in the place of void starkness. He didn't like the feeling of returning to this place; on this side, he didn't know what to do, leaving him frightened and very much alone.

Once again the white-robed man appeared atop the wall.

"Do you understand the difference between that place and this place?"

Alex thought about it. "I think so. In the Garden, we don't have to think or be or do anything. It just is. But on this side, we have to create our own reality."

The man nodded. "The analogy of the apple is the ability to create your reality; to physically manifest your intentions. Regardless of the subtle differences in cultures regarding the elements, all humans were given this gift. When you were in the Garden, everything was perfect. You had no worries, no cares. All was provided. However, when you left the Garden, nothing was provided. You had to make it or find it for yourself. You had to figure out which was the right intention and which was the wrong intention." The stranger paused. "Tell me, Alex. What do you think people have been manifesting since they left the Garden of Eden?"

Alex shrugged his shoulders. "I don't know," he admitted. "But I believe they don't know either. The world is pretty much a mess right now with what people are manifesting."

The man agreed. "And that's part of the problem. Whatever humanity manifests, it's never enough, is it?"

"That's true," Alex replied. "If a toy breaks, I want another. If I eat a piece of cake, it doesn't always feel good. Yet I want more. My Dad always wants more tools. My Mom wants more clothes. It never ends."

The man nodded. "It's because humans are always striving for perfection. Yet, humanity hasn't grasped what perfection is. What is that thing that drives all of you?" Alex shrugged. "Simply put, my boy, it's a feeling that you are all looking for. You're looking for what's in the middle of the star—what humans call Spirit, or chi, or the Great Mystery, or the varieties of names cultures have named this feeling. It's love. Love of having accomplished or created something wonderful and meaningful."

"I'm not sure I understand that," Alex admitted.

"Look at it this way. Every time you do something that's brand new, or something that brings an excitement or satisfaction to you, what happens? You feel good. What is that feel good feeling? It's a reminder of the Garden. But is it ever enough?"

"It isn't," Alex agreed. "I always want more. I want to keep this feeling going forever."

"That's because you're using the elements to manifest strictly for yourself and not for a higher ideal. You're using the elements as a type of drug. It only satisfies you for a little while, until you need to satisfy the craving again."

"Does it ever get to a point where it is enough?"

"Yes it does. That's the beauty of the plan. Your life is a quest for love and understanding why you were created. As an empath, you feel deeply the lack of love in all things around you, especially in the projection from people around you as they wield their limited understanding of the elements. You know there is more and you are driven on a quest—the empath's quest."

HIGHER ASPECT *of* MANIFESTATION

Humans are very good at manifesting. There are hundreds of books on the market that instruct you how to manifest. However, just what are you manifesting? Is it a new house? A new car? A new job? Can you honestly say that what you manifest is enough? How long will the new car satisfy you until you need to buy the newest model? How long will the house keep you happy until you need a change? Will the job keep you challenged or will you begin to think another job will earn you more money? Bring you more satisfaction?

What would happen if you were to step away from the material things you manifest? What if you were to trust that what you need will be provided for? It sounds simplistic, but we can attest that it works. Once you align yourself to a higher intention, you find that your needs are provided for. You begin to learn the right way to manifest as opposed to the wrong way to manifest. You learn to manifest for the greater good of yourself—that is peace of mind, health, and happiness that doesn't come from a box or a new car. Your vibration starts to change and it, in turn, helps change the energy around you. You begin to manifest the energy of being in service to the world around you. You align yourself to a higher vibration of love that transcends words.

The Elements of
Air and Fire

Air

ALEX GLANCED AT HIS WATCH. They'd been in the air for two hours. Three and a half more hours to go before they landed. He idly glanced about at the other passengers. Some were dozing, some reading, a few watched a television program or movie on the small screen imbedded in the back of every seat.

Growing a bit antsy at his confinement, he knew he too could lose himself in reading or watching TV. Yet none of those options appealed to him. Instead, he looked out the window at the huge expanse of vivid blue sky, marveling at the technological breakthroughs that allowed this enormously heavy piece of metal to fly through the air like a bird.

His mind started to wander and he found himself looking back over his life. He'd come to realize all the opportunities that had been presented to him over the years to learn about his empathy. His abilities had grown deeper, but with that growth, also came the awkwardness and uncomfortablility of feeling everyone's emotions, of not knowing if what he was feeling was his or someone else's. It became difficult to navigate a life where he felt he was always on the outside looking in. It would have been so easy to simply live in the woods and hide from everything and everyone. Yet that would have been too unrealistic. Still, he knew he couldn't stand there and accept these feelings all the time. It made him feel apart from everyone, never really belonging. And that hurt because he so wanted to belong.

As the strange man in the dream had told him years before, he always knew there was something more to all of this. But what was it?

The plane dipped to the left and before he knew it, he found himself contemplating the Element of Air as the jet righted itself and continued its effortless flight through the light fluffy clouds.

The four elements that make up substance here on earth and, some believe, the universe, are air, fire, water, and earth. From his readings, Alex knew the Element of Air represented permission to be here on earth, to be alive. A newly born baby would only survive if it could take its first breath of air. Every living creature on earth needed to breathe, including fish in the depths of the oceans, or the trees and plants in the forests. Once permission was taken away, your body ceased to exist and you died.

His years of teachings told him that the first part of manifestation lay in the Element of Air.

He remembered what his druid friend had told him years before. Air is the carrier of information. Smoke carried through the air alerts humans and animals that a fire is burning nearby. Birds communicate with each other through their distinctive chirps that are carried on the air.

It is said in shamanic circles that pine trees communicate with each other over the breezes that blow through their branches.

For humans, the spoken word carried on the air is usually the first means of communication.

Here is where the problem begins.

Through experience, Alex knew there were different interpretations to any given word. For example, he'd grown up with dogs. He considered his childhood fuller because of the various dogs his family owned throughout the years. Yet his friend Billy was the complete opposite. He'd been bitten by a neighborhood dog. Because of his negative experience, the word "dog" represented a deep-seated fear and loathing. This fear and loathing, in turn, caused his energetic vibration to decrease. For Alex, whose experiences were positive, the word "dog" made his heart open with love and his energetic vibration increase.

As an empath, Alex knew this is where many fellow empaths start to get lost in the shuffle of communication. The life lesson of an empath is to understand energy. Energy always teaches true intent by how weak or strong the vibration is that the empath feels in any given moment.

Therefore, by Billy labeling the word "dog" as negative, the very act of labeling the word caused the purity of air to be lost. Instead of just allowing the word "dog" to be just a word, without labels or interpretation, Billy sent out a negative vibration of the air energy. His negative intent would be physically felt by an empath. However, Alex, by just allowing the word "dog" to be just a word, his vibration did not decrease, allowing an empath to simply feel the balanced air energy from Alex.

In a physical sense, the air element teaches the empath the lesson of intention. What is the empath putting out on the carrier of the energy that leaves them? What intention is going out with his or her words?

Alex knew it wasn't the actual words that were important. What was important was the intention behind the words. It was, if you will, the beginning of life.

In the Bible, especially in Genesis, there are several references to situations where "God Spoke." When God Spoke, the intention was that something wonderful was about to be created.

Empaths do the same thing every day with the air energy. Every word we say is the beginning of something else. Yet, it's not the words we need to think about. Rather, it's the energy of the intention we're putting into our words. Intention can ramp up our vibration. By saying the word "dog," Alex was filled with a high vibration of love and affection. Billy, on the other hand, filled his intention with negativity because he labeled the word as something bad.

Another example are the words "I love you." An empath will be able to tell the difference immediately if those words are sincere, or if they are said without the emotion of love behind them.

The trick to understanding the Element of Air and its importance as the beginning of our life lies in thinking about the intention of what we're putting out in the world—not in words, but in energy. Therefore, it doesn't matter if you were bitten by a dog once upon a time. If your vibration is high enough, someone can say the word "dog" and it doesn't matter. It's just a word. It's just a dog. You don't react negatively. However, humans, using their past experiences as their reference point, as well as an incessant need to always label something as good or bad, affect the Element of Air and the lessons it has to teach us.

It is amazing how quickly the energy of air and the intention of fear that is put into it can become stuck in someone for a very long time. Using the example above of the word "dog," the intention of fear that went into that word can remain stuck within a person for as long as they live. However, what if we were to say "dog" with the intention of love in the air energy? Would that soften the person to that moment when they became fearful about dogs?

If an empath pays attention to the energy that is around them, as well as to how they wield their own energy, they cannot help but wonder at the power this energy holds and the possibilities of what it can do to heal. And to hurt.

As Alex continued to stare out the window, he remembered a moment in time when he'd had what he liked to call an epiphany over the Element of Air.

The years fell away and Alex saw himself as a young man in his freshman year of college. By this time, he was already a musician and a member of a band that was growing in popularity. Like many musicians, he decided to try his hand at writing his own songs. At first he thought it would be simple to sit and create. He loved words and his head always seemed to be filled with phrases, random images, and tunes he believed he could capture on paper.

Before long, however, he realized it wasn't as easy as he'd believed. He spent hours, days, weeks, laboring over a song, trying desperately to find the exact words to capture his feelings. His first attempt at songwriting was a love song to a girl he'd begun to see, and it was important that he make this song perfect in every way. He already had the music. Now he just needed the lyrics.

His roommate watched him struggle for weeks. Finally, seeing how agitated Alex was becoming, he sat his friend down.

"You know, Alex, you're killing yourself trying to find just the right word."

"Of course I am!" Alex exclaimed impatiently. "This song has to be perfect."

"Why?"

"What do you mean why? When I sing this song, I want people to feel for Anna the way I feel about her."

His roommate laughed. "Why do you care what people think about Anna? What's important is how you feel about her. And how she feels about you. If I were you, I'd just write the damned song and let people feel what they're going to feel. They will anyway with or without your input." He paused, then continued, "Unless you think writing this perfect song about Anna is going to validate your feelings about her."

Alex was thunderstruck by his roommate's words. Long after his roommate had fallen asleep, Alex still sat at his small desk, pondering what he'd been told. Is that what he'd been trying to do with his fevered attempts to find just the right words to substantiate how he felt about Anna? Was he seeking approval in his emotions for Anna from how the audience reacted to his song about her? Was he trying to elicit from her an even deeper emotion of love since he'd written this song just for her?

The more Alex thought about it, the more he realized that in his efforts to craft perfection, what he was really doing was looking for validation, not only from Anna, but, (and this he hated to admit), his need to be admired and liked as a songwriter, as a musician, as a human being. A part of him relished the thought of people thinking how wonderful and romantic he was for writing this amazing song about the woman he loved. The intention of his air energy hadn't been to simply write a song about someone he cared about. The intention was his need to be liked, to be accepted, to be appreciated. Instead of filling up with the Element of Air in the simple process of giving voice to his emotions, his intention to be validated by others actually lowered his vibration and interfered with the creative process and with the element of fire (which will be discussed later in this chapter).

You see, the intention of air is just to be pure. You don't need to create to elicit a response from others. Since words have different interpretations, you certainly don't need words to prompt a response or validation from others. You don't need to get that energy from anyone. The lesson of the empath is to understand that the energy is always there. You can write, you can create, you can sing, you can do whatever it is that makes you happy with the understanding that as you place yourself in a high flow of energy, you don't muddy the situation with intention. It just is. You'd be surprised how much easier creativity comes to you when you don't force it to be what you need it to be to elicit something from others. The greatest writers and artists have simply allowed themselves to be in the moment, not forcing anything, their intention simply to create. It is at those moments that they are flooded with inspiration. They are a tool of the energy that is always surrounding them. They are able to begin a brand new life—whether it's a song, a story, a poem, crafting a piece of furniture, a satisfying meal, or a flower garden—in that moment. Perhaps this is the muse artists speak of. Perhaps the muse is the permission they give themselves to simply create.

It is true that many make their living out of creating. But in the act of creating, if they allow the energy to just flow purely, their creations manifest that much quicker. This book you're holding in your hands was allowed to be created in the flow of the air energy. The only intention we had was to allow the flow of energy to come forward and find its way to the hearts, minds, and ears of those who are open to these ideas. If these words touch you in such a way, it is because you are at that point in your timeline for it to be so (we will discuss the concept of timeline in a later chapter).

In the empath's quest to understand energy, know that the majority of humanity use words, placing them on to the Element of Air, in order to manifest what they think they need (and what they don't need). Many times this need boils down to a craving to be validated by others. Yet what if we created from a place of just knowing that we are new life every moment and just allow it to flow through us? To manifest, not from a place of control, but from a place of trusting that we get what we need if we open ourselves up to it, without impediment?

HIGHER ASPECT *of* AIR

Think of the Element of Air as a vehicle. As with any vehicle, it needs your permission to move forward. Whatever you put out on to the current of air, as far as intention goes, you are giving what you've put out permission to be. You can give permission for peace, or you can give permission for suffering. The higher aspect of air is to simply be present to the possibilities and responsibilities of air. Therapists always counsel couples to be aware of what they say to each other in the heat of an argument. Words spoken in hate and anger cannot be taken back. They go out on to the current of air because you have given them permission to be there by speaking them. I'm sure most of you reading this have said things that you wish you could have taken back. Going forward, it is helpful to remember the old adage "think before you speak." There is much truth in that. It is also important to remember that in those moments when you have to put an intention behind your words, always understand that your vehicle is going to bring that intention to many different people who are going to perceive it in their own way.

How do you want your words to be perceived? Do you want your words to be stuck within someone forever in a negative way because you needed to elicit a response? Because you needed to be validated in some way? Or do you want to bring love and light and something new to this world that brings us all back closer to that point of perfection—that feeling we all crave deep within us. Words, air, all these things, come back to that initial moment—that singular moment of perfection that we seek. What are you going to manifest with your Element of Air?

In many traditions around the world concerning the elements, the Element of Air is perceived as starting in the East. It is in the East that the sun rises. It is the beginning of a new day. Each day is a brand new opportunity of life. Knowing that the intention of your words can become "stuck" in someone's energy field, how do you want to start your day? What do you wish to manifest at the beginning of your day with your first breath of life? How do you wish to end your day with your last breath of life before you go to sleep? Is it possible to try to spend each day infusing your words from a higher intention of love? Your words may still be misunderstood by others, but you can know that you did your best by speaking your words in the vibration of love and non-judgment and without the need to be validated by others. The energy of that may not be acknowledged by others. But it will be felt.

Fire

ALEX TURNED AWAY from the window just as the stewardess was making her way up the aisle with the food cart. With her attractive blue uniform that conformed to her lean body and long tanned legs, Alex felt a stirring of emotion he'd felt so many times. He recalled when he'd felt that emotion in the past—when he was writing songs, dancing, painting, or simply sitting on a mountaintop. He remembered it each time he started an intimate relationship.

So what exactly were these stirrings?

It was the element of fire, which gives rise to passion. Yet, as he'd learned the hard way, fire and passion have many flavors.

With the rumble of the food cart in the background keeping him company, Alex thought back to the lessons the element of fire had presented to him—lessons that seemed at first diametrically opposed, but were, in fact, very similar.

In his mind's eye, an image sprang up—an image, twenty years before, of a poster advertising a man who was renowned for the drumming circles he ran. It was said that through his drumming and chanting, the audience felt exhilarated and spiritually refreshed.

Naturally, this was something Alex needed to experience for himself. He'd been immersed in the world of spirituality for many years and he was intrigued that this man—a fellow musician—could mystically touch his spectators.

It just so happened that the drummer was promoting his newest CD by performing at a new age shop near where Alex lived. He immediately signed up. When he arrived at the shop on the night of the event, he felt conspicuous as the only male in a room filled with women.

He stood at the back of the room that had been set aside for the concert, watching two young men set up both Native American and African drums in a semi-circle around the chair where, Alex assumed, the musician would sit. Women began to gather in front of the small stage, their anticipation electrifying the air. The current was strong; the fire element of passion was slowly igniting.

Alex knew this energy. He'd felt it himself many times when he was up on stage. There was a language of physical yearning that took place between the audience and himself. When he was the center of their projection of the fire energy, it felt good. He felt empowered. Tonight, however, the fire energy wasn't directed at him. In fact, the women completely ignored him as they waited for the star of the evening to appear. It piqued an unexpected jealousy in Alex—he wasn't accustomed to being ignored by the opposite sex. Considering he was the only male in the audience, he thought at least one of the women would talk to him. But they were all engrossed in trying to sit as close to the stage as possible.

To walk off his irritation, he wandered around the store. There was a curtained-off area near the rear, and he watched the men who'd set up the drums leaving and entering through the curtains. He knew this was where the musician and his entourage were waiting. Feeling a pull, he wandered over and stood near the curtains, pretending to look at the boxes of Tarot cards on display. He heard the sound of voices. He was ashamed to be eavesdropping and considered leaving, but something was keeping him rooted to the spot. He soon discovered why.

"You've got a full house out there," one of the voices replied. "Beautiful women in the front rows and a healthy check for an hour's worth of work."

The drummer snickered. "Now you know why I do this. I don't even believe in all this spiritual mumbo jumbo, but you can't beat all that money or attention from the ladies just by banging a stick on a piece of animal skin." He burst into laughter.

Alex felt his stomach tighten with disgust. He'd been to drumming circles before; he knew how sacred they were. Yet this man was knowingly violating the sacredness of the ritual because of his addiction to the energy he was getting from the audience—an addiction he was probably not even aware of.

Alex wanted to leave. He knew this man's intention had ruined any sacred spirituality that might have existed. Yet, a strong feeling came over him that he needed to stay. He'd learned long ago to listen to these feelings, even if they made him uncomfortable. So he made his way to the last row where he'd have a good vantage point of both the stage and the audience.

As soon as the drummer appeared, the women focused on the feeling of fire that was beginning to grow.

He had to admit, the drummer wasn't much to look at. With his shoulder-length brown hair and long, narrow face, he wasn't what one would call handsome. Yet as soon as he began to gently beat one of the Native American drums, a magnetism rose to the surface, a smoldering sexuality that spoke to the women. Alex watched in fascination as the drummer gathered to himself the passion energy of the ladies.

He only gave enough of his own energy to keep the women hungry for more. It was an energetic dance of give and take—the drummer teasing just enough with his fire energy to manipulate the women into releasing all their energy to him.

As Alex watched this, a horrible realization hit him.

Is this what I do when I'm on stage?

He understood all too well how intoxicating and seductive that energy felt. It was addicting. How could it not be when he held such power in his hands? Now, however, watching the drummer dance the dance that he too was guilty of, he recognized how corrosive it could be.

His lessons in the element of fire continued.

Soon after the experience with the drummer, Alex and his band performed at an outdoor fair in New Hampshire to celebrate Midsummer. It was a successful show and when they were done, he and his band mates, along with members of the audience, sat around the stage, enjoying the night air. Nobody seemed in a hurry to go home. On an impulse, Alex took out his guitar. Rather than sing the hard rock songs Alex usually sang with his band, he opted to sing old folk songs and ballads.

The night air grew still as Alex's lovely tenor voice made its way across the Element of Air to his small audience. A movement caught the corner of his eye and, without missing a beat, Alex turned in time to see a young woman appear out of the darkness. He was immediately struck by her ethereal beauty. It was almost as though a wood fairy had materialized before his eyes. She sat at his feet and looked up at him, a shimmery light reflecting off her white-blonde hair from a campfire someone had set up nearby. Her shy smile showed off deep dimples in her cheeks and her eyes held a seductive glow. Alex found himself filling with fire energy, marveling how, under her intent gaze, he seemed to be singing better, playing better. The essence of the physical expression of fire and passion were becoming more enlivened.

Although she sat quietly and demurely, Alex felt as though she were enveloping him with her entire being. What he didn't realize was that she would require something in return.

His small audience was forgotten as he focused his entire attention on her. He sang to her. He played for her. Try as he might, he simply could not take his eyes off her.

To his astonishment, she abruptly stood up and walked off into the night. He felt her energy pull away from him. He felt bereft. He had to get that energy back. He had to get her back. He stopped playing and put his guitar down.

"Hey dude, don't stop," someone called out. "That was a beautiful song you were playing."

"Sorry, but I've got to go after that girl. It's something I have to do." All he could think about and focus on was that girl. Who was she? Where was she?

Desperate he'd lose her, he rushed down the path he'd seen her take.

He stopped short when he found her lingering near a grove of trees. His heart gave a leap as the passion increased. Was she going to lead him into the grove? Would they make love surrounded by the nature he cared for so much?

As if in a dream, he slowly approached her and took her hand. Looking into her eyes, he asked, "Who are you?"

She smiled at him and when she spoke, her voice was soft and sweet. "It doesn't matter. All I know is that when I'm around you, I seem to know more about who I am."

"Me too!" Alex exclaimed, unable to believe how in sync they seemed to be.

She gently traced his lips with her fingertip. "What are we going to do about it then?"

With his heart hammering in his chest, Alex bent down, ready to take her in his arms and kiss her. He closed his eyes and was about to touch his lips to hers when he heard a rustle from a nearby bush.

"What the hell do you think you're doing? That's my girlfriend you're coming on to."

The voice shattered the magical moment. Alex swirled around to see a tall, thin man stomp out of the bushes. He was dressed in black leather and with his face contorted with rage, he exuded an unmistakable aura of danger. Alex didn't care. The fires that had burned as passion now exploded into a raging inferno of jealousy and anger. The two men confronted each other as the girl unobtrusively slunk away into the night.

Alex never felt this enraged before. This man had destroyed an enchanted moment with the girl of his dreams. He wasn't a fighter by nature, but he was ready to rip this man to shreds.

His band mates and organizers of the fair arrived in time to stop any violence from taking place. With difficulty, they managed to separate the two men. While a few stayed with the man in an effort to calm him, the others pulled Alex away. When they were far enough away, they told Alex the truth. To his chagrin, he discovered that the "girl of his dreams" was famous for doing what she'd done to Alex. She used her fire energy to seductively lure men away from their friends where her boyfriend would beat them up under the guise of protecting her. It was a rush for both of them as they manipulated the energy of fire to garner it from others.

His lessons in fire continued.

Whenever Alex sat down to create a song, he felt the passions of the earth rise up and spark inspiration. He felt the passions of the earth when he sat on a mountaintop and experienced the primal essence of the trees and animals around him. By allowing the higher vibration of fire to envelop him, Alex felt the very cells in his body become alive.

It brought him to a memory of a trip he'd taken out to Colorado with friends. He'd allowed himself to be talked into going on a trail ride. He'd never been on a horse before and he didn't know what to expect. His friends were experienced riders and he quickly found himself completely out of his element. Holding on for dear life and expecting to die at any moment, the horse galloped through fields, jumped over streams and raced up and down steep hills. At the end of the ride, instead of feeling angry that his friends had almost killed him, he was surprised to find that he'd never felt so alive in his life. Feeling the fire of the horse beneath him and the passion of his own survival, his body and mind tingled with an exhilaration he'd never felt before.

Fire energy can be so easily misused. Passion is one of the strongest physical emotions humans possess. They can be overpowered by it, as Alex was when the girl's boyfriend confronted him. Many murders have been committed in an "act of passion." Passion allows people to override others to get what they think they need. The color red, most associated with passion, is a very powerful emoter of energy. Many interior designers will not use the color red when decorating an office because red is perceived as an aggressive color. In the psychology of color, it has been known to actually reduce analytical thought.

However, as with the other elements, people consciously or unconsciously seek to get this energy from others. They will deliberately elicit a response, or put out an intention to gather energy to themselves. As with air, water, and earth, the fire energy is always there. All you need to do is tap into it.

Passion isn't so much an act of doing things passionately as simply being in the fire energy and allowing it to flow through you. Unlike air, which is a carrier, fire is a transmuter. It either creates or destroys. It is up to you to choose. As an empath, you can use the fire energy to change an aspect of yourself by symbolically shedding the old skin, destroying those thoughts or actions that no longer serve you. Many spiritual teachers will recommend writing down on a piece of paper those aspects of yourself you wish to rid yourself of, then burn the paper with a match or in a fire.

The passion of fire can also be used to fuel creativity. As you fill up with this passion, you become more alive. Your energetic vibration rises and you are filled with light. You can see this light in the faces of those who are doing something they love. They beam with this light. By tapping into the purity of the fire element, which always surrounds you, you now have the ability to receive its gifts of creating something new and wonderful, or destroying an old habit or thought or behavior that is hindering you. However, keep in mind that if you take this energy from others, you also take the intentions they have infused their energy with.

The choice is up to you.

HIGHER ASPECT *of* FIRE

Fire is that passion that comes from the earth. It fuels the urge to create, to change. You never need to elicit responses from others to get this energy. It is always there. Just as fire creates, it also destroys, but destruction can be used constructively to cleanse away so something new can come in. When you connect to your fire energy to create and transform, you allow a light to shine on the physical opportunities of change and newness to come into your life.

Yet, what is it that starts the fire burning? Is it us feeling this energy from another? Feeling our own fire energy and wanting to add more fuel to it by adding that energy from another, not realizing we are capable of creating that fire to take it to unimaginable heights without the use of another's energy? Is it a look from someone that provides the spark? Does that open the door so the fire is sparked? If someone does something for us and we are feeling validated in that moment, is the fire sparked then?

It comes back to taking this energy, these feelings, from each other. What triggers that? What starts that process? So many turn off their fire energy in fear they will be taken the wrong way. Many people use their fire to get from each other. They are not honoring the gift of fire—the gift to create, to remove those things from us that no longer serve us by the day, every day. The fire energy is always there. Use it to forge new things in the fire—new passions, new abilities, so that we can begin to create a newer us.

The Elements of
Water and Earth

Water

THE PLANE DRONED ON. Alex reached for his bottle of water. As he did so, he slowly became aware of the crying of a baby a few aisles down from where he sat. He overheard the baby's mother trying to hush the child, but he continued to cry. Turning around, he watched the woman get out of her seat with her baby held to her chest and head towards the bathroom.

Turning back, Alex glanced down at his water bottle. Before he could stop himself, lessons regarding the element of water loomed up before him.

Empaths are constantly questing for that which makes them feel good within themselves. Many times this quest finds them entering into relationships that are less than validating, but the ability to feel love and the need to have love from another human being overrules their senses. Even when they physically feel the falsity of their partner's emotions, they still plunge ahead. The Element of Air carries the words of love they desire to hear; the element of fire fuels their passion for another. The element of water presents the lessons of emotions.

And what a hard and painful lesson that was.

As with many empaths, Alex believed marriage would help him feel better about himself and fill up those emotional holes he carried. It would validate him as a human being by having another person love him.

After several failed relationships, Alex met Carrie. She was pretty and vivacious, and his heart melted every time he saw the love she had for him sparkling in her eyes. Before long they were inseparable, and his mind started to turn towards marriage. They were at an age where their friends were getting married and starting families. Why should they be any different?

Yet whenever he thought he was ready to propose, he felt an uneasiness in the pit of his stomach. A warning voice whispered in the back of his mind that Carrie was not the one for him. Something was off. Something wasn't right.

Alex refused to listen. He chalked up his uneasiness to typical jitters. It was a huge step to commit to and be responsible for someone else. And what about kids? Once they started coming along, he'd be responsible for making sure they were nurtured and cared for and taught the proper values. That in itself would make anyone nervous.

At least this is what he told himself. The truth went deeper. His need to belong, his need to feel love, his need to be validated as a worthy human being by that love pushed him on. He convinced himself that the Universe had brought Carrie to him and put this whole relationship together. He therefore proposed, Carrie accepted, and before he knew it, he was married.

He realized, too late, that it wasn't the Universe who had put this all together. He had, because of his need to feel within himself the feeling of the energy he craved.

Still, for the first few months they were happy. Alex laughed at his initial nervousness. He'd been right. He really had just been suffering from pre-wedding nerves.

Then reality set in. The closeness he'd shared with Carrie seemed to be slipping away. He scrambled to find an explanation that would explain her increasing distance. They were struggling to make ends meet. Maybe that was the reason for her coolness. He worked harder, putting in additional hours at work to bring home a larger paycheck.

It didn't help.

Now began the journey many empaths take—the weaving, twisting, and navigating their way through the circuitous path that emotions take them on.

Alex couldn't admit there was something wrong. He couldn't admit that Carrie was falling out of love with him. To admit to that would mean he'd made a terrible mistake. Worse, it would mean he was incapable of being loved. So he continued to bury his emotions deeper and deeper. Arriving home after work and feeling her dissatisfaction, he would slip into a neutral state of not feeling her emotions or his own. He did not realize this was certain death for an empath—the detachment from the experience of feeling.

Whenever Carrie tried to sit him down and tell him their relationship wasn't working anymore, Alex swiftly interrupted her. "It will be okay," he insisted. "Just give it a chance. I promise you, it will all work out."

Of course it didn't. If anything, their relationship got worse. In response to his refusal to accept the inevitable, Carrie started to drink. She stayed out frequently with friends. Despite the obvious signs, Alex continued to deny there was something wrong. He didn't want to feel the rejection, the disappointment. As an empath, he knew those emotions would drown him. So he buried them deeper.

Then, one day, Carrie walked out the door and never came back. The marriage unraveled as quickly as it had come together.

They got a divorce.

Throughout the divorce proceedings, Alex still could not bring himself to look at what happened between him and Carrie, what his emotional part had been in the break-up. He buried the feelings deeper, determined to make the proceedings as easy as possible and not get bogged down in blame, guilt or fear.

His coping mechanism was to convince himself they'd been too young to get married. It was one more brick in the dam he was building around all those unresolved emotions he wasn't ready to deal with.

Yet he'd been scarred by the experience. It took him two years to try again.

At one of the shows he and his band played, he met Jessica, a tall brunette whose intelligence matched her beauty. An undeniable spark ignited and they quickly moved in together. At first, it was wonderful. He felt validated by her love, her attentiveness to him. She introduced him to a world of art and museums and fine cuisine, while he introduced her to the magic and serenity of nature. Determined not to make the same mistakes he'd made with Carrie, he made sure they had enough money. He did all he could to spend enough time with her.

However, once again the relationship ground to a halt and it ended. It left Alex in an emotional tailspin.

What was he doing wrong? No matter what he did, he couldn't seem to hold on to a relationship. With each break-up, he was overcome with emotions he didn't want to feel. He wished he could continue to bury these feelings of rejection, of unworthiness, of . . .

A light bulb suddenly went off in his head. Was that the issue? Was that the answer to his failed relationships?

Had he been trying so hard to make everything perfect for his mate, that he'd denied his own emotions?

He thought back to his childhood—to those times when he'd heard his parents arguing. They were always loud and scathing to each other, not caring who heard their angry words flung at each other like sharp weapons. As a sensitive child who felt the emotions behind their words, Alex wanted to shrivel up into a little ball and disappear. Could his parents' explosive confrontations have caused him to vow he'd never feel or provoke that kind of response in his own relationships? Each time those hurtful emotions bubbled up, he repressed them. With each relationship that floundered, he buried them deeper and deeper. The problem was, emotions won't stay buried forever. They will rise up one way or another.

When a third relationship failed, Alex found himself unable to repress his emotions any longer. Years of trying to bury them now made them insistent to be dealt with. Unfortunately, they usually demanded to be heard at very inopportune moments. He'd be at work and a random song on the radio or a word from a co-worker would cause uncontrollable tears to well up. He'd feel himself coming apart just going to the grocery store.

Alex knew he had a choice. Despite the problems of dealing with everyone else's emotions, he knew that when he went neutral not to feel the "stuff" of others, he was actually blocking his own sense of feeling. He could try to live his life in an incomplete way by denying his emotions, which wasn't working anymore. Or he could allow the water to flow and cleanse him of all the hurt he'd kept bottled up inside for so long.

As an empath, it is part of your journey to understand that feeling what you do is part of the process of learning what it means to be an empath. Think of a dam. It is built sturdy to keep the waters back. But if the pressure of the water isn't released periodically, all that concrete and steel will break and the water will burst forth in all its ferocity. The same happens to humans if they deny release of their emotions. It builds and builds until one day there's an explosion. It may take something as simple as someone giving you a wrong look and before you know it, your emotions are running away from you. It wasn't the look that triggered the flood. It was the accumulation of emotions over the years, denied its natural release, that decided on its own when to burst forth.

As an empath, you've probably at one time or another tried to hide from your feelings. Whether the feelings are yours, or someone else's, it doesn't matter because you still have to deal with them. However, what if you allowed those feelings to come out little by little instead of erecting a dam that will eventually break? What if you were able to "unplug" from the emotions of the feelings and just see it for what it is—energy? How many of you have buried a hurt or a slight from childhood only to have it resurrect itself in your adulthood? Are you still carrying the baggage of a childhood hurt or trauma? How many times have you sought validation from others because years ago you weren't validated by a parent or an authority figure?

If you watch a child, they go from emotion to emotion. They feel happy, then cry, then feel happy again. What if you allowed yourself the same luxury? Repressed emotions are the cause of many illnesses. That energy has to go somewhere. Wouldn't it be better to use the element of water to allow that energy to flow through you than have it bounce back on itself and eat away at you?

Constricting your emotions means that the energy contained in the element of water is not permitted to flow. If you dam them up, then the explosion of emotional waters will take charge of your life and choices are not as easy as they could be. Imagine trying to make decisions in the middle of a flood.

Remember that the ability to allow energy (and emotions) to flow is the lesson of water. It simply flows. If you judge an experience, it constricts the flow. An experience is just an experience until you judge it otherwise.

The Universe has an uncanny way of teaching the truth of energy. What else does this energy of water do to your manifestation process? What do you bring into your life and push out of your life?

You use your feelings, your water energy, and the intention of what it means and doesn't mean as a barometer in your life. In other words, if you feel energy that is uncomfortable, you immediately go into the thought, "Oh, it's going to be a bad day." You then get your wish—it's a bad day. It's as if you manifested it by adding that intention to your water energy. By the same token, how many times have you said, "It's going to be a great day," and you put forth that thought process into your water energy? Sometimes it is a great day. However, don't forget, there's a big world out there waiting to have its own emotional experience with all the people surrounding you, having their own issues with their own water energy and their own elements. Suddenly, *wham!* As an empath, no matter how hard you try to make it a good day, no matter how hard you try to keep your emotions good, you still go into that barometer—oops, something changed; I'm feeling this lousy energy. You lose your ability to keep your good feelings going. The trick to navigating your daily life isn't so much the barometer of the energy—is it good or bad. It's more about the flow. Allowing those emotions, those feelings you feel to flow in any instance. It doesn't matter if it's your emotions or someone else's. You're feeling it anyway. At some point, your protection techniques are going to break down because you're denying who you are—you're a feeling human being who has the gift of feeling everything.

Understand, it's not the barometer thought process that has to go away. That simply allows you to identify in any given moment if what you're feeling is comfortable or uncomfortable. What's important is to allow the flow of emotions to continue unimpeded—the energy of flow—the energy of water flowing through your body. Not every day will be a good day. Some days will be awful. But if you can allow the energy to simply flow through you, without labels or stories attached to it, you will find yourself riding the waves without drowning.

HIGHER ASPECT *of* WATER

Water is a cycle. Water flows down from the mountains, into the streams, which then empty out into the oceans. Water then evaporates up into the clouds where it returns to the earth in the form of rain. Like the element of fire, water can destroy, but it also cleanses and creates in the fertileness it brings to the earth. It works the same with feelings. Whenever you try to dam up something or try to take control of a natural process, it doesn't work. Things are displaced and not allowed to grow. Fertility loses its way. Allow the purity of emotions to come to you. You don't need to label it or hang a story to it. Just allow the emotions to flow through you. If it helps, visualize a stream of water flowing within your body, carrying away all those things that have angered or hurt you. This is a form of grounding. As you do that, know that humans are feeling creatures. You were created to feel. It is not weak to feel. It is weak to think we can control everything, including emotions.

ON THE PLANE, the mother's attempts to quiet the baby hadn't worked. He was crying louder. No matter what she did, she couldn't quiet him and her frustration and embarrassment was growing. Passengers were becoming increasingly upset and agitated. The tension was rising. And Alex, as an empath, was feeling all of this. He felt himself getting caught up in the anger, the annoyance, the sheer irritation of everyone around him. His stomach tightened and his chest hurt.

I've got to pull back. If I don't, I'll just be adding *my* gunk to this already crazy gunk. For a moment, he had a mental image of a giant ball of goo careening down the aisle towards him. The image caused him to chuckle and he felt a slight release from the tensions he was feeling.

But it wasn't enough.

He knew the best way to move all this emotion was to climb a mountain or sit with his back against a tree. This connection to earth always moved the energies out of him. But he was 37,000 miles up in the air. What was he going to do now?

Alex had a habit of always carrying in his pocket a small piece of smoky quartz he'd found atop a mountain. It served as a reminder of his connection to the earth. He pulled it out and held it tightly in his hand. He felt the energy shift and start to flow out of him, but it wasn't fast or strong enough.

The intensity of the energies around him grew until he found himself struggling to catch his breath. He was on the verge of a panic attack. Was he not grounding fast enough because he was in the air? Because he was surrounded by too many people? He remembered stories on TV of people panicking in planes and trying to break down the plane door. He hadn't reached that point yet, but he was beginning to understand how they could feel that way. The stone that he'd relied on so many times as his reminder of the earth energy in the past wasn't enough. If he was ever going to fly again, was he going to have to carry a smoky quartz the size of a brick?

He took in deep breaths of air and through his panic, he had a knowing of a tree. Then flowers and grass—all the things of the earth. He smelled the comforting fragrance of the fir trees. Felt the crunch of pine needles under his boots whenever he walked through a forest. He went into their energy and felt himself becoming calmer as the energy started to dissolve.

That got him thinking. He didn't actually need to be physically connected to the earth to ground to it. Although he was 37,000 miles above the earth, he was never truly separated from it. Because, in truth, he was the earth. When he was in his mother's womb, she had eaten products from the earth—plants, meat, etc. Those, in turn, went into him. Every cell in his body came from the earth. As a part of the earth, he shared in its energies and in its choices. Part of that choice was to be like the trees and the rocks and the animals who were happy

being what they were. A tree has no problem being a tree. A dog has no problem being a dog. A rock is happy being a rock. It's people who have a hard time being people.

In that moment, he had a choice to make. Could he sit on this plane and shun the feelings of annoyance and frustration from the other passengers who were threatening to overwhelm him? Could he go into fear and try to shut down? Or could he take what he'd learned from the elements? Could he take the feelings of everyone around him that were being transmitted through the air, the fire of everyone's anger and using the water element, have them flow out of him? Could he then ground out these emotions through his feet using the element of earth?

Alex closed his eyes. He no longer fought the emotions that threatened to overwhelm him. Using the element of water, he pictured a stream of water move through him, taking all the emotions with it. He felt his feet tingle as the energy flowed out his toes. He started to relax, the tension oozing out of him. His body was a vehicle of his experience, not only physical, but also emotional and energetic.

In tapping into the pureness of the earth energy, he knew there was no heaviness to this energy. The earth was a perfect system that always worked in balance—each part of the energy feeding, nurturing, protecting, anchoring; each a spirit unto itself, but all working together in absolute balance. This energy had no need to be different; there was no desire to change itself to suit the situation. Humans, on the other hand, were constantly reinventing the moment and the situation in whatever context they needed the energy to be. They believed it was their own personal will that had control over the energies they were feeling.

Suddenly Alex had a realization. What if the knowing he'd learned of these elements, coupled with human will, were part of the understanding of why humans even exist? What if the purpose of the earth energy is to always remind us of what to be in balance means—a balance where nothing is better or different or impure? Of just having the experience of being with an earth that works in perfect harmony?

He went back to the basic teachings of earth energy. Even though humans insist on duality—black vs. white, good vs. evil, etc.—the truth was that things really weren't good or bad. They were just being at any given moment. It's the labels people put on things that gives the energy its intention. Intentions and labels are learned from our past—things we've been through—things we believe to be truths. Things we believe we must control. The control is the problem.

The earth works perfectly in balance. A tree grows, sheds its leaves, goes dormant in winter, and begins the process of growing new leaves in the spring. The river knows it needs to flow. The air knows it needs to blow through the tree branches. The fire knows it sometimes needs to burn away the old so the new can be born to continue the process of life. People, however, have lost this sense of balance. They constantly try to control the situation. In this need to control, they go into the card file in their brain created from past experiences and begin to create energies that are less than perfect because of these past experiences.

Why this control? Why this uncomfortability in our bodies? Why this barometer of dictating what we feel and what we see? Through this need to control, we try to gather more energies from others, from things outside ourselves. It is these false intentions and labels that make the energy empaths feel uncomfortable.

Through his experiences, Alex knew the power of trying to ground out uncomfortable energies through eating or smoking or doing drugs. Unfortunately, this type of grounding never lasted because it wasn't real. In those moments when he reached for an exterior item to make himself feel comfortable, he was forgetting how connected to the earth he truly was.

We all have moments where we feel uncomfortable in our physical selves. It's as if our skins crawl, or we're seemingly stuck in a place of perpetual negativity where we feel as though we're physically walking through muck.

Things of the earth—trees, stones, etc.—have no need to move uncomfortable energy because they each know they are connected to the earth. They haven't forgotten they are of the earth. They each hold an energy that makes them remember they are connected, not only to the earth, but to the heavens as well, because something created them. Each thing on this earth works as a battery—a storage of energy that is comprised of their story, their experience.

Let's take a peach as an example. A peach contains stored-up energy from the sunlight that helped create it. This energy, working much like a battery, is then ingested by humans. Eating the peach feels good. It tastes good. You've consumed the pure energy the peach holds within itself.

Now take tobacco, an item that is from the earth. When people smoke, they take in the energy of the smoke. In that moment, they become the tobacco plant. They are grounded. They feel the essence of the earth energy going into their system and for a brief moment, they are a more perfect battery. Unfortunately, it is the tobacco itself that is doing the grounding, not the person. And once the energy of the tobacco dissipates, they no longer feel grounded—which is why they reach for another cigarette. Consciously, they are not remembering that they don't need the tobacco to ground themselves. They have that ability within. But they have become addicted to the feelings the false grounding of the tobacco gives them. It starts them on a treadmill of tobacco addiction—a need to recapture that grounding over and over again.

The same can be said with holding certain stones. Stones are connected to the earth and, as mentioned earlier, connected to the Creator, because something created those stones. Part of its purpose is to help anchor us. When you hold the stone, you feel grounded. You feel its energy. What happens, however, when you put the stone down? Its energy dissipates and you're back to your own forgetfulness of your connection to the earth.

This can certainly be seen with food. Particular foods make us feel comfortable in our skin. Why do we eat chocolate cake or ice cream? Why do we crave comfort foods? Why is it so difficult to give up sugar? Sugar provides a quick energetic feeling within yourself—it tastes good. It makes you feel good in the moment you're consuming it. Then, as with the stone and the tobacco, once the energy dissipates, you're back to where you started from.

All these things serve its purpose. They are trying to teach you how to be connected to the earth. Whenever you judge an experience, it takes on a life of its own and becomes more physically grounded in your body. If you look at something as bad, you feel its heaviness. If you look at something as not fair, you find yourself in a swamp of unfairness that you feel in your physical body.

Yet, if you step back and just experience the energy without labels and intention, you can feel that balance without tobacco, or sugar, or holding a stone. Like them, you also hold that connection to the earth, as well as the heavens, because something created you as well. When you find that balance for yourself, you work in tandem with the earth. You are in sync with its energies. You no longer need an outward object to ground. You hold the power of it within you.

By getting back to a sense of calmness and acceptance, Alex was able to project his calmness to the baby. After a few minutes of enveloping the baby with his own calm energy, the youngster began to quiet down. Soon it was no longer crying. Alex knew that if he'd remained in his agitated state, his agitated energy would have gone out, joining with the rest of the agitated energy in the plane and growing exponentially.

It brought to mind a biography of the late Robert F. Kennedy he'd recently seen on television. In 1968, while campaigning for the presidency in a black neighborhood in Indianapolis, news reached RFK of Martin Luther King's assassination. When he asked his aides if the crowd knew, he was told they did not. He was advised not to tell them because riots had already broken out in other major US cities and the police could not guarantee his safety. He nevertheless made the decision to share the sorrowful news. Climbing on to the back of a truck, he told them of King's murder. There were gasps of horror, yet Kennedy kept calm and spoke to them, saying, "For those of you who are black and are tempted to ... be filled with hatred and mistrust of the injustice of such an act, against all white people, I would only say that I can also feel in my own heart the same kind of feeling. I had a member of my family killed, but he was killed by a white man."

Indianapolis did not riot. Was it his calmness, his compassion for their pain that kept them from rioting? He was able to elevate their horror and anger by keeping his own horror in check. He was being who he was, taking the road of love and compassion. He spoke with sincerity from the heart. He contained the violence simply by being.

HIGHER ASPECT *of* EARTH

Just be. Whenever we go into bad/good, light/dark, life/death, we put an intention of fear behind our emotions. How many trees or stones are in fear? Things just are and work in perfect balance. Humans are the ones who try and control and interfere with this balance. When we put our label on to something, it produces that energy of fear. What earth teaches us is that everything works together with each of the elements playing its part to keep us in balance. However, what would happen if we simply allowed things to be the way they are? What sort of energy would you be putting out then? By remaining calm, as Robert Kennedy did, you have the opportunity to ground out another person's emotions. As an empath, you will feel it whether you want to or not. Your choice is either to allow the energy to be by not judging it and allow it to ground through you, or you can label it and add your own emotional intention to another's emotional intention and watch it explode. Know that as an empath, you will be brought to situations in order to learn the lessons the elements have to offer. Knowing how to navigate these lessons then brings you to the wondrous gift of the quest to understand what this thing is that we call existence.

What Is the Quest?

WHEW. WHAT A RIDE THIS HAS BEEN!

Not only was he riding on a plane, but Alex realized, he was riding on a wave of remembering the hard lessons he'd undergone throughout his life. He was grateful for having learned the lessons the elements offered: how the vehicle of air could so easily project a heaviness out into the world, how fire could be such an unbelievable creative force, but in order for something to be created, something else needed to be destroyed. Even this plane ride had served as a perfect opportunity to revisit those lessons—the baby crying serving as a reminder to release emotions through the element of water, and grounding his and the baby's energy through the earth element. It made him realize who he really was. It also made him wonder if it was possible that this is what life was really all about?

Is our life designed as opportunities to experience?

As Alex mulled this over, his eyelids grew heavy. Before he knew it, he slipped into a deep sleep. Unexpectedly, he found himself at the long, endless black wall again. It had been years since he'd been here and so much had happened since his last visit.

Looking up, he smiled. There was the familiar figure of the man with the luminescent white robe and cherubic face, sitting on top of the wall, munching away on an apple. The man looked down at him and waved.

"It's been a very long time since I've spoken to you. You've grown quite a bit."

"Well, it has been over thirty years."

"Thirty years? My, my, imagine that. Seems like a blink of an eye to me." He leaned forward. "So tell me, my boy, with all that you've experienced so far, are you finally getting it? Is it all making sense?"

Alex carefully considered his question. "Yeah, I think it is. I've come to a great many conclusions about a great many things. Even this plane ride has served as a bit of a lesson for me. There were moments I wanted to jump out the door. But I remembered the energies of the elements and it's helped me."

"Good thing you remembered your lessons and decided not to jump. How in the world would you ever explain landing on your feet after a 37,000 foot drop!" The man chortled while Alex wondered if he was actually serious. "Well Alex, your life has been what I would call the quest of the empath. Your experiences in life have been opportunities to understand how things really work. In fact, as an empath, you've had no choice but to experience these things as they unfolded."

Alex snorted. "That's for damn sure. I feel everything that happens, whether I want to or not. There are days I feel like I'm wading in a swamp or stuck in a huge soup pot. Yet, although life might be easier getting through if I hid away, I'm always driven to get back out into the world."

"Why do you think that is?"

"Because the more I do that, the more I realize I've gotten a pretty good handle on all that crazy energy out there by paying attention and not judging it. By understanding the power of what we manifest and put out there—"

"Stop right there!" the man exclaimed, thrusting his hand forward. "I want you to understand something. The initial understanding of the elements that you've just figured out is the ability to manifest your individual will. It's the power that manifests your point of view. It's the declaration of the word. There's all this conjecture that the world is good or evil, yet what is good and evil? Light and dark? Good or bad? They are opposites. It's called duality. This idea of duality drives you to choose one or the other. When you were on the other side of this wall that you're still trying to get back to, you were the elements. You had no need to manifest anything. Suddenly in your curiosity or what some people believe was an act of defiance, you chose to take on this power as your own."

"What is this power you're talking about?"

"You've been seeing it on this airplane. You've been seeing it your whole life. It's to declare, to intend, to impose, to project, and to create. The problem is, when you were on the other side of this wall, it was all done for you. You didn't feel duality because there wasn't any. There was no good or bad. It wasn't needed. Everything was perfect. It was what you would now call 'bliss.' Yet, you chose to turn away from perfection. It bored you. So now you're on that side of the wall. Now you are choosing for yourself."

"We're not doing a very good job of it, are we?" Alex replied.

"Because you are making choices from a place of lack. You don't understand what it is you need to manifest. You never had to do it before. Now, when you wield this elemental power, you are making your own choices. But here's the point I want to make. Whenever you make your choices, it's never enough, is it? It simply never is enough in your own mind."

"So why go through all that hassle in the first place?" Alex asked.

"Because it's part of the quest to experience, to learn how to get back to that place of perfection. It's the beginning of an energetic ascension. It begins with duality. I need to say this to keep myself safe to hold power. I need to hear this to feel validated that I am worthy. I need to be angry and wield this fire energy to keep others at bay. I need to create to bring to me significance. As you can see, it becomes a big vicious circle because it's never enough. You are constantly reinventing the wheel, playing the game twenty different ways. Is it true that when you manifest something like a new car, is it ever enough?"

"No. I always want more."

"Is it true that when you have money in your bank account, which should make you feel safe, you still feel it's not enough?"

"No, I always want more."

"So what drives that?" The man pointed his finger at Alex. "This is what you are being taught. This is part of the quest of the empath. Every human being is driven to feel good or bad. Naturally, their quest is to always feel good. It is those moments when you feel the most uncomfortable, however, that teach you the most profound lessons. Take that crying baby as an example. It wasn't pleasant for anyone to hear it crying. It certainly wasn't pleasant for the baby to be crying. Yet look how much you figured out about energy by having that baby cry."

Suddenly, Alex saw several instances in his life where things had fallen apart, moments when he'd had to be strong. Instances where he'd felt so uncomfortable that he wanted to scream. Yet he hadn't given in. He'd been able to step back and not judge the moment and the energy had ground out of him.

My God, my life really is an energetic quest.

"The quest," the figure continued, "is to experience energy better, stronger, more loving. What you humans think of as love is just a vibration. You label it love—love of things, love of people, love of energy. They're all experiences within your mind, your body, your spirit, and your emotions. Each offers its own lesson. As you learn that lesson, you climb to higher vibrations of love.

"You manifest with the elements. You draw to yourself something you think you need, or push away something that makes you feel uncomfortable, rather than simply experience the energy for what it is. That's why it's never enough. Look at the history of humanity. It's never been enough. You've always sought more—more attention, more power, more territory, more possessions. And so it continues."

Alex realized that it wasn't so much the experience of the energy itself, but also what the energy taught. As an empath, he knew it had nothing to do with the mechanics of why things happened. The experiences have to do with feeling. Maybe in all this, there was an opportunity to get to the truth of who we are and why we were brought into existence.

ENERGETIC EXPOSURE

As an empath, many of you spend so much time in your heads wondering why, how come, what if, how do I just feel better? You question yourself constantly— what if I had done this or done that? Would the outcome have been different? Believe it or not, this is the beginning of the process for many empaths, the beginnings of understanding the mechanics of why you feel what you feel. In order to try and feel better, many of you reinvent yourselves, barter parts of yourself away, try to hide. But what are you really hiding from? It isn't so much you're hiding away from what happened. You're hiding away from the experience of the feeling of the energy you either lost or received. Yet no matter what you do, there will always be another situation you will go through, another love, another loss, another feeling, another hurt, another happening out in the world to give you an energetic experience. Why? Because all these things are teaching you something bigger. Sooner or later, every empath goes through this. It's part of this crazy ride we call life. But if you understand these things are happening to teach you, it becomes easier to bear. Because the end result is worth fighting for.

Be Careful What You Wish For

ALEX AWOKE FROM HIS NAP and rubbed the sleep from his eyes. Wow, this was turning out to be more than he expected when he boarded the plane. He sat back in his seat and went over his dream.

He thought back to how he'd wielded the elements in his life, the things he'd manifested into being. They all eventually lost their luster as the fantasy he'd wrapped them with faded. No object was going to make him feel like Superman, nor give him the validation he'd once craved so much. And if it did, it never lasted. He'd then become obsessed with how he could keep it going. Did he have to buy more things? Change relationships? Change friends?

There always seemed to be one more energetic lesson to learn.

Finally, as he learned the lesson each of his experiences presented, he came to the realization that he could feel like Superman and get his validation without manifesting anything. No outside object was going to make him feel good inside. No person was going to completely fill up his desire for validation. Why? Because that energy was within him. That energy was always within him. It didn't come from others' intentions or judgments. It didn't come from their own emotional baggage. It was there, in its pure form, for him to tap into. With that realization came a peace and calm that money and things could never buy.

As Alex thought over these things, he noticed an unexpected tightness growing in his belly. He checked his energy and realized it wasn't his, though he was certainly feeling it. Before long, he heard a muttering in his ear. Glancing to his left, he noticed the man sitting next to him. He looked to be in his early forties and dressed in an expensive business suit and tie. His face was contorted in anger as he stared down at his iPad in disgust.

"Really? Are you kidding me?" he seethed under his breath. He slammed down the leather cover over the iPad and sat back with a thud, a curse on his lips. Realizing what he'd done, he glanced over to Alex. "Hey, sorry. Shouldn't have lost my temper like that."

"Sounds like something really upset you."

The man turned in his chair and studied Alex. He thought Alex seemed innocuous enough, dressed in jeans and a shirt. But there was something about this stranger, a peacefulness that reached out to the businessman. Unaware of what he was doing, but feeling the need to release his pent up tension, he started unburdening himself.

"I've been on the road for two weeks attending meeting after boring meeting. I swear, I'm sick of holding people's hands. Seems everybody these days needs their hands held. They're certainly getting paid enough to do their jobs, but I still have to go in and fix all their damned mistakes. Now I find out my boss has scheduled me for an overseas trip."

"Overseas? That doesn't sound so bad."

"It is when it's your son's seventh birthday party. My wife has been planning it for months. She's got the whole shebang—a clown, pony rides. You name it and she's done it. I carefully planned my travels so I'd be there. I've already missed his fifth and sixth birthdays," he added darkly.

"Tell me, have you always wanted to be successful?"

The man looked at Alex as though he were crazy. "Who doesn't?"

Alex took a moment to feel the energy of this moment he was having with the businessman. Was he pushing this man to the edge of an energetic cliff? Was the man ready to hear what he had to say?

I need to trust this is happening for a reason. I'll continue to provide myself as a sounding board for this guy.

"Has it made you happy?" Alex asked.

"Huh?"

"Let me put it this way. In order to be what you believe represents success, you manifested this busy lifestyle."

The man's gaze turned into an angry glare. "Why am I even talking to you?"

Alex felt the man's anger. In an effort to defuse it, he used the lessons of earth and water to move and ground it out. At the same time, he filled himself up with the high vibrational energy of air to envelop his words with love so the man could feel Alex's words coming, not from a place of ego or condescension, but from a place deep in his heart.

"Listen, I mean no offense. Hear me out. You've got nothing to lose."

"Just don't give me any mumbo jumbo about manifestation, whatever the hell that is."

"Fair enough. Let me put it this way then. Your interpretation of what success means is to have lots of money, right?" The man nodded. "Nice suits, a big house. The ability to afford to give your son these huge parties. But making all that money usually means using up a lot of time to do it. A large chunk of that time is making sure you keep your boss happy, your shareholders happy, your competition off kilter so you can continue to make money and keep everyone happy. Everyone, that is, except your family." Alex leaned forward. "The sad part is that you brought all of that into existence by manifesting it. You thought it into being. Now of course, a lot of hard work went into it, but I'll bet that you became so obsessed with what you interpreted as success that it became the focus of your entire being."

"You're right," the man admitted. "It did."

Alex felt the man's energy soften. "At what cost? Tell me, how do you feel when you get that big paycheck?"

"I feel like I have purpose. I've reached my goal."

"But is it enough?"

"What do you mean?"

"Is that big paycheck enough?"

"Of course it isn't. There are always more bills to pay."

"But it's more than just the bills, isn't it? The money gives you power, doesn't it? It gives you prestige. It makes other people look up to you. But when is it enough?"

The man narrowed his eyes at Alex. "What are you? Some kind of nutty guru who thinks money is evil?"

Alex laughed. "Far from it. I enjoy money as much as the next person. I'm not saying you shouldn't go out there and earn what you can. The money makes you feel good for a little while, but now you're sitting here, feeling frustrated and angry. Not a very good manifestation, is it?"

The man looked at Alex in surprise. "I just got shivers over what you said. Are you doing that?"

Alex shook his head. "I'm just sitting here, having a conversation with you."

"Mmmmmm."

The man wanted to stop talking to Alex. This strange man was making him think of things he didn't want to think about. But he felt compelled to continue. Against his better judgment, he asked Alex, "So tell me about this manifestation you keep bringing up."

"It's okay to earn money. We have to eat. We have to have shelter. However, is it possible that this manifestation thing we do as humans—and I speak from experience when I tell you all humans manifest—can it be done for a more balanced purpose? For example, what is it that you want? You want to feel powerful. You want to feel wanted. You want to feel desired. These are all things you can have without money."

"That's not true. I need to feed my family. I need to take care of them. They need to feel protected. I need money for that."

"How are they protected when you're constantly gone making money? Constantly worrying about your job? How are they feeling then?"

"Well, they do complain I'm not around enough. And when I am around, I'm distracted by business."

"Let's look at that. You've gotten what you wanted. But do you really want it? How does it make you feel right now? Your life of success of what you thought you were supposed to do is not enough. Your family isn't happy because you're not there. You're not happy because you're not there. Your boss will be unhappy because you want to be at home with your family. Your success isn't fulfilling you anymore."

"It must be because I'm doing something wrong. My father was obsessed with becoming successful. He—" Suddenly the businessman stopped mid-word. Alex filled himself up with the purest elemental energy that he could manifest. Instinctually, he knew he needed to manifest the perfect container for this man to feel safe enough to share, to go deeper to release whatever it was he was holding on to within him. It was a subtle type of healing Alex was quietly offering him.

After a few moments, the man resumed speaking in a subdued voice.

"I just realized something. My father was a success, but not in the way he wanted. He actually planned on buying up land to develop. He knew that was the way to make a load of money. But my mother was a timid woman. She was terrified of not having enough money. So even though it was a sure bet, she wouldn't let my father buy any land. It was always a deep disappointment to him."

"And now you're doing what your father couldn't."

"I think I am."

"So what you've done is taken on your father's wants and desires to be successful and turned them into your own. You've manifested what others say is a successful life. But you've lost a balance. You've sacrificed precious time with your wife and children to what you've been taught is success. And now you're paying the price. You thought it would bring you happiness. Make you feel whole. But it's not working anymore, is it?"

The man shook his head.

Alex leaned forward. "Be careful what you wish for. Because you just might get it."

FINDING BALANCE

We spent so much of our life chasing the proverbial carrot, thinking that if we catch it, we'll feel better. We'll have success. We'll find more love, have more things—all those items that if we can just hold them in our hands, will make our life all better. But is it so? Do we really know what to manifest that will make us truly happy? Advertising agencies spend millions telling us that if we use their products, we'll have the perfect life. We'll be more beautiful. We'll find more love. We'll be more abundant. We'll accumulate more things that, at the end of the day, will only elicit an energy that tells us it will never be enough. Why? Because in their playing to our ability to manifest, we are manifesting from their thought process, not our own. It is their things that are being put in our space. As though we are being led blindly to having their manifestations of convincing us that what they have will fix us, thrust down our throats. Therefore, the "be careful what you wish for" is part of the lesson. It is part of what we're learning in our ability to manifest. What is it that we truly want to manifest and how does that work? How does that move us forward? How does that bring us closer to the quest of finding that which is so elusive? That feeling that what we have is truly enough. That we are truly happy. That we are finally in balance with what we have and with who we are.

The Timeline

THE BUSINESSMAN went back to his iPad, pensive, more relaxed than he'd been since he'd boarded the plane. What the stranger next to him said made sense. Too much sense. Changes were needed. And he would ponder Alex's words as he set about making those changes. Not big ones. At least not overnight. But enough to give him what he really wanted—to be with his wife and family and savor those moments he was now throwing away and would never get back again.

Alex smiled inwardly. He didn't smile from a place of ego, or from a sense that what he'd done validated him in some way. He smiled because he knew this moment with the businessman had been meant to happen. He'd felt its energy, as all empaths do, just as he'd felt it was time to take this trip to Arizona.

It was all part of his timeline.

Alex rested his head back against the chair and closed his eyes. He remembered trying to explain the concept of the timeline to Zoey many years before when she'd called him, upset that she'd received yet another rejection slip on a fiction book she was trying to pitch to a literary agent.

As far back as she could remember, Zoey had dreamed of becoming a writer. She first "published" a story in second grade in the school paper and she'd been hooked ever since. She'd studied writing, majored in English in college and, for several years, met with numerous agents and editors in an effort to get her fiction published.

"I've come close so many times," she lamented to Alex. "I've won prestigious writing contests, I've had agents love my work, yet at the end, it's snatched away from me. I don't get it. What am I doing wrong?"

"You're not doing anything wrong," Alex replied. "You're just not surrendering."

"So in order to become a published writer, I'm supposed to throw my hands up in the air like in those old war movies on TV and yell out, 'I surrender'?"

"Only if you like being dramatic."

"Great. That helps."

Alex chuckled. "Let me ask you a question. Have you had moments in your life where no matter what you had, it was never enough? You always felt you wanted more?" Zoey nodded. "By the same token, have you had moments when something came along that fell into place perfectly? It was as though you had no choice in the matter—you just had to walk this straight line towards something that beckoned you?"

"Yeah, I did. A few years ago, I woke up one morning knowing that was the day I needed to look for a condo. It came out of nowhere, but I knew I had to follow through. I picked up the newspaper, saw an ad for an open house and drove straight to the place. As soon as I walked in, there was something about the condo that told me it was mine. There were ten people there, but I ended up buying it." She grinned. "It was the first place I ever owned and I always felt safe and comfortable there." She looked at Alex. "Now that I look back, it did seem as though I was on auto-pilot. I just knew what I had to do and I did it without thinking."

"You surrendered to the process. You didn't wake up fighting the feeling you had to look for a condo. You didn't second guess every step you took that day. You didn't push buying a condo a month before or a month after. It was part of your timeline to buy that place on that particular day. What if our lives are made up of these series of lessons—a quest, if you will—where initially we do things to see if it's ever enough? Eventually, we realize that in order to make our life work, we surrender because if we don't, we're constantly faced with the prospect that no matter how much we manifest from a place of our own will, it's never enough."

Zoey rolled her eyes. "You're going all new agey on me again."

Alex laughed. "Okay, let me explain it this way. As you know, for many years I was part of a band. We were getting huge. People were traveling from all over the country to see us. One summer I sat down to write a song and suddenly six songs poured out of me. They were there with no effort on my part. If I tried to do that now, it would be nothing but a struggle."

Zoey nodded. "I just read an article where Phil Collins from Genesis said that whenever he was in the right space and was open, the songs just flowed into him, while David Bowie said every song he wrote was a painful experience."

"Now, let's look at that. What if our lives are a set of lessons that get us to surrender because, by surrendering, we're led on to our life path? When things that are supposed to happen according to our timeline unfold, they unfold effortlessly, perfectly."

"I'm still not seeing how this all relates to my writing career, or at this point, lack thereof?"

"I'm getting there. Just hear me out a bit longer. As the success of the band grew, all I wanted was to be famous. I pictured myself winning Grammies for my songwriting, for best album of the year. I wanted to be up there in the pantheon of music superstars, like the Beatles and Nirvana. I wanted our album to be on the top ten list for a bazillion years, like Pink Floyd's *The Dark Side of the Moon*. I was determined to manifest this into being. I became obsessed with every step of the process. I constantly had to know what the fans were thinking of us. We got ourselves a manager and I remember continually asking him what he thought of us. This incredible need for validation drove me nuts, but I couldn't help myself. And you know what? Everything I'd wished for, everything I'd fought hard to manifest started to happen. We cut a demo tape and the record companies immediately sat up and took notice. We reached a point where we were actually booked to do a European tour and were ready to sign with a major music label. Then, in the blink of an eye, it all fell apart."

Zoey's eyes widened with surprise. "Really?"

"Really. Through a set of weird circumstances, the band fell apart overnight. We lost the tour, lost the contract with the record label, lost our manager. I fought tooth and nail to get it going again, but I couldn't."

"What did you do?"

"What else could I do? I felt as though my whole life had just collapsed. I had no choice but to try and figure out just what the hell happened. I went to see my aunt, who was a very spiritual lady and spilled my guts out. Like you, I asked her what I was doing wrong. Why did I come so close to something I wanted so badly, only to have it fall apart? And you know what she said?" Zoey shook her head. "She asked me if I was finally ready to learn."

"Kind of anti-climactic," Zoey replied.

"She was right. I needed to get my stubbornness and ego out of the way so I could begin to learn the lessons of what my crazy life was all about."

"So what is this great wisdom you're about to bestow upon me?"

Alex smiled. "It's quite simple. You're empathic just as I am. And like me, you have the ability to sense the vibration of any given moment. You know in an instant if you're feeling good or not so good, correct?"

"Correct."

"Let's take that a step further. When you're so fixated on manifesting something from your own needs, you don't sense the vibration of the moment, do you?"

Zoey thought about it, then shook her head. "I don't think I do."

"How do you think you would feel if you began to manifest, not from a place of your own needs, but from a place of a higher need?"

"What is this higher need?"

"It's a method to the madness."

Zoey frowned. "Now you *are* going new agey on me."

"Maybe just a little. But it makes sense once you understand the plan. Back to my story. So there I was, my music career in ruins. Everything I thought would fulfill me was gone. It's said that many times what drives a person into the spiritual need to discover what their life is all about is when they hit rock bottom. I can attest to the truth of that statement. I couldn't have gotten any lower than I felt at that moment. Thanks to my aunt, I started attending spiritual classes, trying to comprehend what had happened. I thought music would make me happy. But just what is happiness? Is it even attainable? Is there some way to get there? Should I pray more? Go on more spiritual retreats? Sit on a mountain and meditate?"

"You're a pretty happy guy," Zoey commented. "So obviously you found some kind of answer."

"I did, and when I did, I couldn't believe how simple it was. You see, I began to realize that all those years doing the music thing hadn't been a waste. They served to bring me to something else. Without the music, I never would have learned about the vibration of sound. I was a shy kid growing up, but without the band, I never would have learned to get up in front of a crowd of people and be comfortable with it. Without feeling the energy of the audience and my own energetic reaction to it, I never would have learned how to change that energy by changing my own. I learned that I didn't need to fulfill myself through the attention of others. I learned that my life wasn't all about the music. The music simply served as a vehicle to get me to where I was supposed to be. I realized there was a method to the madness."

Comprehension spread over Zoey's face. "I see. All those lessons you learned through your time in the band helped you to begin to become the spiritual teacher that you are now."

"Exactly."

"Wait a minute though. Are you saying that it's a waste of time to have aspirations?"

"On the contrary. All I'm saying is to listen and feel the energy. How many people go into a career because it's expected of them?"

"Quite a few. It leaves them unfulfilled."

"It's all right to have a job that serves a purpose of allowing you to eat and have a roof over your head and support a family. However, you need to find other ways to energetically fulfill yourself. To listen to what the energy is trying to tell you and teach you. As soon as I stopped fighting to become a famous musician and surrendered to the moment, I learned an incredibly valuable lesson."

"Which is?"

"There is more."

"More what?"

Alex sat back in his chair. "What is the one complaint you always hear from empaths?"

Zoey laughed. "The same one I have. I get overwhelmed feeling everyone's emotions and want to hide."

"Now, what if I were to tell you that those moments when you feel overwhelmed serve as lessons? What are you feeling? What are those lessons? You're feeling the manifestations of the elements from all the people around you. You're feeling their need to be right with their words, to get power over you, to be clever. You're feeling their passions, their need to exercise what they want in this world. You're also feeling their inability to release whatever emotions they're holding on to, and you're also feeling their use of the earth energy in their obsession to be validated. All that stuff is and never has been enough. As you grow spiritually, sooner or later you start to have energetic experiences that you learn from. When you judge people, your energy tanks. When you don't judge people, your energy stays in a good place. Experiences like that. As you gain an understanding of energy, you start to feel the 'more'. It has nothing to do with people. The 'more' has to do with the energy that propels you forward on your timeline. You get to the place where you surrender to what that is. Not what people dictate what your life is, or even your fearful place of what you think it is."

"Okay, I get that. But what is this timeline you mentioned?"

"The timeline is another word for a person's life path."

"Then why don't you use the word 'life path'?"

"Because what I've seen and experienced is that things happen in your life according to when they're supposed to happen. Some people call that divine timing. But it has to do with the concept of time. Things happen in their own time."

"So does each person have their own timeline?"

"Yes. All the beginning lessons were about survival and our human experience of manifesting. However, the human experience sooner or later realizes it's not enough, because what we're really manifesting is getting energy from each other. It has nothing to do with getting bigger houses, or succeeding in a band, or being a published writer. That's all a way to get over on someone else, to get energy from another person. If I have more passion in my life, I'm getting that from others. They're filling me up. If I'm clever with my words, look at me. Aren't I special? It's called significance."

"But don't we get energy from things?" Zoey asked.

"Yes. But ninety percent of the time, the energy you're feeling is what a person placed on the thing. So the things that you do get energy from, the things that remind you that there's more, are nature, the trees. Why do trees always feel fine? Why do stones feel fine? Why are empaths drawn to stones or those things that have nothing to do with people that make them feel fine? There's the clue. The elements and how to manifest with them on the timeline helps you to understand how being here in this life works and why you go through what you go through. What I want you to understand right now is that in the moment when you're feeling bombarded, you have an option."

"I do?"

"Yes. You don't need to become a victim of the moment. You have options. You can choose to hide from the moment and be a victim to it, or you can take a step back and look at what the moment is trying to teach you."

"How did you figure out this timeline?"

"It started when I began to do psychic readings for people. How was I able to see their future? Why was it that I could see things that did in fact happen? How could I see things that were going to happen that, no matter how hard I tried, I couldn't change them from happening? That got me thinking. Things were supposed to happen in a person's life, no matter what. It was there to teach them. That's why it's sad when a person thinks their life is ruined because their choices didn't work out. Instead of seeing it as a failure and holding on to that energy, see it as a set of lessons that will get you to someplace else."

"Like your attempt to being a rock star actually giving you the skills to be a spiritual teacher."

"Exactly. I guarantee you, all the things you're learning in your choice of becoming a fiction writer is going to help you in the future. Just surrender to the process and see where it takes you."

Those words drifted back to Alex as he sat on the plane. They were as true now as they were several years before when he'd spoken them to Zoey. He'd had an option when the baby started crying. He could have hidden from that energy and blocked it out. He could have put up all sorts of protection so he wouldn't need to deal with the passengers' reactions to the baby crying. As he'd learned, protection actually isolates a person from the energetic experience and a chance to learn from that energetic experience. What he did instead was open his heart to be more fully present in that moment. He took the higher aspect of the moment and helped change the energy by grounding it out, using all he'd learned from the elements to help him. The same was true of the businessman. He could have ignored the anxiety he was feeling from the gentleman and let the guy spin his wheels. The old Alex would have done that. But because of what he'd been through, what he'd learned over the years, he could now offer the man a different perspective from his own life experiences. His timeline and the man's timeline intersected at this particular point in time, giving him the option to share what he'd learned with the man. The man, in turn, had felt the energy vibration of the moment, probably for the first time in his life. By speaking to the businessman, Alex placed the kernel of potential change. Now it was up to the man to follow through. The choice was his. But it wouldn't have happened if their timelines weren't supposed to intersect at that moment and if Alex hadn't chosen the higher aspect of that moment.

He glanced across the aisle to Zoey, her nose buried in a book as usual. She'd taken his lesson to heart and surrendered to whatever her timeline had in store for her. She stopped pushing to get her fiction published. She continued to write, honing her skill with words, but let go of the obsessive need to be published.

A few years after her conversation with Alex, she finally did become a published author. All the lessons she'd learned writing fiction now helped her to write nonfiction. Everything she learned about the publishing industry now helped her craft the perfect proposal to get her work picked up by a reputable publisher. Her books on spirituality captured people's hearts because, like Alex, she was sharing life experiences that resonated with people all over the world. She was imparting the hard lessons she'd learned over the years, helping the reader appreciate the fact that, no matter where they were in the world, they were not alone in what they were feeling and experiencing.

When Zoey looked back and thought about her conversation with Alex regarding her timeline, she realized how perfect it had all been. If she hadn't gone through the years of learning the art of writing, of meeting with agents and publishers, and learning how the world of publishing works, she never would have reached this point in her writing career. As she told Alex when she signed her first book contract, "I did finally get published. Only I never imagined in a million years it would be in nonfiction."

Alex smiled. "It's where your words were needed most."

SURRENDERING *to* YOUR TIMELINE

Your life is made up of a series of lessons that make you who you are. Sometimes you don't get to fulfill a lifetime wish, but what you've been through is probably getting you ready for something bigger. If you look back over your life, you'll notice that things happen in a certain order to get you to a certain point. This is part of what we call a person's timeline. Every person has one. This timeline is what holds your lessons, your destiny. It is a map that you follow—many times unknowingly. You really only notice the map of your life when you've experienced enough to be able to look back and see where it has taken you. But it's there. And you can make it easier to follow by surrendering to it. By surrendering to any given moment, you take your will out of your own way and allow the bigger picture to unfold. Alex didn't become a famous rock musician, but he found deeper fulfillment in becoming a spiritual teacher. Zoey didn't become a successful fiction writer, but her books on spirituality have fulfilled her much more than fiction ever could have. And, more importantly, it's helping people make better choices in their own lives.

As an empath, you always have a choice in how you react to any given moment. You can hide away and become a victim to what you're feeling. Or you can try to learn just what the moment is trying to teach you energetically. What you once considered failures are actually teaching you to reach for the higher energy. For example, how would you feel if you ate vanilla ice cream several times a day for months? You'd lose your taste for it. It would become stale. Take that example and apply it to what you manifest over and over in your life. Relationships that become stale. Reaching success only to find it doesn't fulfill you. So many in the entertainment field implode once they reach what they thought they wanted. They find they can't take the fame. They can't keep it going. It's not fulfilling. The businessman on the plane is a perfect example of people manifesting what they think they need, only to discover they don't want it when it happens.

You know you've reached the higher energy when things unfold without effort on your part. When what you're doing feels so right. When you don't need to push and force something to happen. By surrendering and learning the lesson of any given moment (and knowing that life is a series of lessons to be learned), you find yourself fulfilling your timeline and being filled with a higher energy that is without human wants, but instead filled with the purity of your purpose and why you're here in the first place.

Energetically Courageous

"We are preparing our descent into Phoenix. Please return your seats to their upright position and fasten your seatbelts."

Alex immediately felt a shudder in the energy on the plane. As an empath, he felt the anxiety of everyone around him rise as they prepared for the landing. Rather than shut down or try to block it out, he allowed himself to settle into the energy—to stay present and allow it simply to be.

He glanced around at the passengers and was taken aback when he suddenly realized he could physically see colors around each of them swirling in their individual auras. He had seen these before in his life, but never in this intensity. They were the colors of the rainbow, but the colors were muted, muddy. Perplexed at what he was seeing, it quickly dawned on him that the muddied colors were actually telling him where an individual's vibrations were. He felt the energy of the colors and realized they served as a barometer for where each person was energetically in their lives.

He looked over to Zoey and noticed that the colors surrounding her were brighter, more vibrant. It made sense since she'd spent years healing her issues and embracing the lessons her timeline presented to her. He peeked at the businessman next to him and saw that his colors were not as dull as the others. Again, this made sense since it seemed he had taken Alex's advice regarding his life to heart and had spent the rest of the flight making decisions that would favorably impact his future. Those decisions were reflected in the now brighter hues to his energy field.

And here I just thought I was going to be bored on this five-hour plane ride. Yet, I've learned so much about energy and how far I've come on my own path trying to understand my life and how all of this works. Goes to show you never know what's going to happen or when.

One lesson stood out from the others. In the past when bombarded by everyone's divergent emotions, he would have quickly shut it all out, trying his best to hide from it all and putting up all sorts of protection so he wouldn't need to feel it. But now he was open. In fact, he focused on becoming even more open to feeling everything that was going on in each passenger's energy field. Just as he'd done with the crying baby and the businessman seated next to him, he stayed with the energy to see where it took him.

In so doing, he'd become energetically courageous.

In nature, he'd always noticed how the colors surrounding the trees and the animals were vibrant and almost twinkling in its swirling, brilliant tones. That was because nature had no problems being nature. On the plane, however, the swirling colors were reflecting the fears and anxiety the passengers felt at the prospect of landing, or the problems they were living through in their lives. Everyone knew take-off and landing were the most dangerous moments on a plane and he felt that fear vividly. Yet he held his space and rode the fear in its waves and eddies.

He looked down and saw his own colors expanding throughout the plane. He understood at once that as he held space for everyone, he was, at the same time, independent of their drama and anxiety. He was simply present, without judgment, the center of calm in a whirlwind of apprehension.

Another knowing occurred to him. This whole plane ride, this whole trip to Arizona in fact, was part of his timeline. It was a matter of being in the right place at the right time to help the businessman, to ease the child's crying, to look back over his life and realize the lessons he'd learned about the elements and how far he'd come. Despite being a spiritual teacher for a number of years, Alex understood that a successful teacher will always be a successful student. Learning never ends. This plane ride was proof of that.

My realizations on this plane are going to come to fruition on this trip. How do I know that? I don't know, but my spider sense is telling me to be aware and see how everything unfolds.

As he continued to expand his energy, he realized that he was experiencing where his energy began and ended. It was a complaint he'd heard so many times from other empaths, including himself years before. It was easy to become so swamped with feeling all the energies around them that they lost their boundaries. They didn't know where they began or ended. They didn't know if it was their energy they were feeling or someone else's.

For the first time in his life, Alex was conscious of his energetic boundaries. He didn't feel closed in or as though he was going to explode. In fact, by not judging or trying to figure out what or why things were going on—in other words, just letting the energy be—his own energy was changing. It was growing stronger. It wasn't being weighed down with his own interpretation of what was happening. This again was part of his timeline—to feel this and to understand it. He was learning profound truths through his experience that he could pass on as lessons to others.

Everyone's timeline is safe, no matter what. We just need to be in it and learn how to navigate it.

But how to navigate it? He mused over that for a moment, and the answer came to him. He didn't need to get his energy from others. He didn't need to manifest from a place of fear or protection. He didn't need to hide away in a closet to escape what he was feeling. All he needed to do was embrace the moment, to no longer be a victim to it, but to sit back and see what lesson the moment was presenting. The choices he'd made over the years were all based on whether the choice made him feel good or not so good. Many times, the choices were not made in truth—they were material choices. For example, choices to look better for someone else, choices to eat junk food because it made him feel good in that moment, etc. But once he started to make choices in truth, for example, choosing to forgive a person or a past hurt, the energy actually flowed and he was able to move past the stagnancy of his life. He aligned more to his timeline.

He abruptly sat up as a realization hit him. That was what this whole plane ride was about. It wasn't just a way to get from Point A to Point B. It was a way to make him aware of his timeline, in fact, of his destiny.

Destiny doesn't always have to be this huge, momentous thing. Destiny can be made up of moments when you quietly realize things that change your way of thinking, or make you consider something you may never have considered before. Like this plane ride. He thought, *I boarded it never imagining that I'd be leaving it a different person. I put into action all the things I've learned about the elements, about being present, about not judging, but just allowing things to be what they need to be without my directing them to be a certain way.*

His epiphany had an unexpected bonus. Now when he glanced at people, he saw small geometric figures in their energy fields. Before he could ponder the meaning of those, the plane touched down with a jolt and the colors and figures abruptly disappeared.

Gathering his things, Alex knew he'd be seeing those figures in the not too distant future.

After disembarking from the plane, the little group gathered together and made their way down to the luggage carousels and the rental car dealerships. They'd arranged to lease a van for the week that would accommodate the four of them and their luggage.

"So, once we get the van, where do we go? I'm ready to get this energy party started!" Zoey exclaimed excitedly.

"There are some Anasazi ruins I thought—" Alex started, only to be interrupted by one of the more vocal of the group.

Cora met Alex a year before at a new age gathering and gravitated towards his teachings regarding energy and empathy. She had red hair and a round freckled face and possessed a personality that was large and forceful—so forceful in fact, that she had a tendency to overwhelm others with her willpower.

"I told my family I'd bring back souvenirs. I want to get my shopping out of the way so I don't have to worry about it for the rest of the trip. There must be a mall near here we can hit."

"Why buy everything now? You may find something nicer somewhere else," Zoey pointed out.

"If I get it done now, it's one less thing I have to worry about."

The group tried to reason with Cora, but she was adamant. She wanted to go shopping now.

Alex kept silent as he observed the change in energy amidst the group. Where before the energy had been calm and filled with the excitement of the trip, it was now turning dark and muddy like the passengers' energies he'd observed on the plane. The Element of Air was being wielded in such a way that Cora's words were becoming more strident, more demanding. He felt the energy of the ladies growing smaller, withdrawing from Cora's onslaught. He saw how, in an effort to keep the peace, they were giving away their elements of air, fire, water, and earth while Cora exerted the elements to get her own way. They were submitting to what he knew as community manifestation—where one person's will is so strong, they are able to rope others into their way of thinking. He'd been subjected to it himself many times in the past when he too had been reluctantly sucked into another person's suggestions.

Observing once again how interesting energy dynamics were between people and how he'd have to continue to pay attention as the trip progressed, he decided to give into Cora's demands.

They found a mall and spent hours idly standing around while Cora set about buying her souvenirs. By the time they reached their hotel, the women were frustrated that their first day in Arizona had been a complete wash. Keri, one of the newer members of the group, was particularly vocal about it later on when she and Alex were alone.

"Why did we even invite Cora along?" she seethed. "She always does this, and we always give in."

"She's a perfect lesson for you," Alex replied.

"Yeah? Like in how not to strangle someone who ticks you off?"

Alex laughed. "That's one lesson. Another lesson, and this one less violent, teaches you how not to become the energy and desires of someone else."

"Are you saying we basically became Cora's energy and wants?"

"I'm afraid you did. You got so sucked in, you forgot who you are. You lost your boundaries of where you begin and end because you allowed yourself to get pulled into her energy. You kept the peace, but gave away a piece of yourself."

"Not much of a bargain."

"For the rest of this trip, pay attention to the energies, not only of yourself, but of the others around you. I have a feeling we're all going to learn some really great lessons along the way."

The next morning Alex awoke with a resolve that he wasn't going to allow anyone to dictate the day's events. They'd come to experience the different sites and he was going to make sure they stuck to that itinerary, or at least to what the timeline presented to them.

After showering and changing, he went down to the lobby to await the ladies. He wandered over to a rack that held tourist brochures advertising the various sites to visit. One in particular caught his eye. He picked it up and saw that it was a brochure to the Homolovi ruins.

The Homolovi State Park included seven separate pueblo ruins built by both prehistoric peoples and the ancestors of the Hopi, between approximately 1260 to 1400 AD. He felt an energy shudder through him and he knew they had to go there. He wasn't sure why, but the pull was too strong to ignore.

When the ladies arrived, he showed them the brochure. Zoey too got a shudder while Keri and Cora were struck by the beauty of the pictures. Deciding to visit the state park, they ate a quick breakfast, then piled into the van. Unlike the day before, Alex noticed the energy among the group felt good. Once again he caught glimpses of the colors in their energy fields and saw they were bright. The hard feelings caused by Cora the day before had apparently been forgotten.

Arriving at the park, they were all astonished to find they had the place to themselves. Although it was spring, the state parks were usually crowded with visitors, despite the growing heat of the day. Alex instinctively knew this wasn't an accident. Something was going to happen, though he didn't know yet what it was.

Around them were ruins of what had once been houses of the ancestral Pueblo Indians. Stretching into the horizon was the flat brown landscape of the desert, giving the area a sense of desolation. To Alex's eyes though, there was a beauty to it all. Rather than desolation, he felt a deep sense of peace and serenity.

As they picked their way around the ruins, he saw his hunch was right. Something was happening. The energy surrounding them began to pulsate—first slowly, then ramping up in intensity. It felt as though they'd walked into an electrical current.

Alex separated himself from the group and slowly walked around, trying to figure out why he was feeling this overwhelming feeling of high intentional vibration. He felt himself growing lighter and lighter, as though at any moment he could float up into the blue sky. Interspersed in the energy was a feeling of profound sacredness.

"Hey, come here! Look what I found! It's a *kiva*."

Alex turned in time to see Zoey beckoning everyone to where she stood before a large, perfectly round hole dug into the ground.

"What's a kiva?" Keri asked.

"According to the exhibit marker, it's a place where religious ceremonies were held."

Without hesitation, Alex hurried back to the group and stepped down into the center of the kiva. "Let's all sit in a circle," he instructed.

The group did as he asked. The energy immediately began to increase. Before he could fully grasp what was happening, he began to see shapes, symbols, peoples from the past flash before his eyes. He instantly knew that somehow, sitting in the kiva, his timeline had intersected with a timeline from the past, and he was seeing the ancient Anasazi people. Reflected through the images, he saw his own group, saw their colors increase in intensity. He saw the geometric figures in their auras surge in size.

Was it possible they were accessing the ancient prayers and the energies of those prayers of the ancient peoples through their own empathic sensitivities or from the manifestations of the elements?

As if in answer to his question, he heard the low humming of prayers in his ears. He smelled the aroma of long ago fires. His experience showed that the teachings of the shamans were right—time is not linear. If you know how, you can access the past, present, and future at any given moment.

It was happening to him now. And it was amazing.

"Hey, you're not supposed to be in there."

Alex was abruptly thrust back into the present. He blinked his eyes a few times and looked up to see a park ranger standing above them, his hands on his hips and his eyes snapping with fury.

"Sorry. We didn't know we couldn't."

"There are signs posted everywhere."

The incredible energy they'd all been feeling fell apart instantly as the ranger's anger assaulted them. They quickly scrambled out of the kiva and mumbled more apologies before taking their leave.

"Well, that didn't go well," Keri replied as they drove away.

"Actually, it went exactly as it was supposed to," Alex answered. He shared his experience and was delighted to discover that a few in the group had experienced the same thing.

"At first I thought it was my imagination," Zoey said. "But then I realized it was too real. I felt as though I was really there all those centuries ago. I even smelled the smoke of the fire and had a sense of the roof that used to be over the kiva."

"I didn't see what you saw, but I could feel the top of my head tingling," Keri replied. "I felt as though I were surrounded by people. I even peeked to see if there was anyone there, but there wasn't."

"Well, there was, but they were there in spirit," Alex pointed out.

"That's amazing! So where are we headed to now? I'm eager to see what else I feel today," Keri exclaimed excitedly.

"It's a little over two hours to the Grand Canyon. I don't know why, but we need to go there next."

They continued to discuss their strange experience in the kiva as they drove along the highway. Both Cora and Keri had never experienced anything like that before and they marveled at how the energy felt.

"It was as if I no longer felt burdened by any worries," Cora explained. "I felt so light."

"That's because your energetic vibration increased. You didn't judge the moment, or try to make it something other than what it was. You surrendered to the experience," Alex said. "In truth, you had no choice. That feeling of what you think love is was being given to you, making you feel safe to surrender."

"Where did it come from? Nobody was there," Cora persisted.

"Something was there. Something in time and space was placed there. Could it be it was put there for someone at some time to come along and feel it?"

"You mean, someone like us?"

"Could be."

Alex felt a flicker of Cora's ego begin to grow. He quickly added, "We're not special. No one in this van is special. It's simply that we're open to these possibilities and these energies, especially since we're learning to embrace our empathic experiences. There will be others like us who go to that kiva someday and experience what we did."

The ladies grew quiet as each considered his words.

The miles flew by and soon they were pulling into the parking lot of the large visitor center located on the southern rim of the Grand Canyon. A huge sprawling building filled with exhibits and the history of the canyon inside, Alex was instantly mesmerized by the symbols that were painted all over the walls. He felt a pull to walk towards the right, past the exhibits, past the displays and information desk. Ordinarily he would have stopped to look at all of these, but not today. Not with this energy pulling at him. He didn't know what he was being pulled towards, but as he'd learned long ago, he knew there was a reason for it. The reason became evident when he turned a corner and found himself standing before a huge sand painting in the middle of the floor. He knew the Navajo tribes used them for healing and this one had many of the symbols he'd seen on the walls when he'd entered the visitor center. As a child, he'd been drawn to books detailing sand paintings and their meanings. Now, here he was, standing in front of one. It was awe inspiring.

He slowly walked around the display, looking at the carefully arranged colored sand and eagle feathers that surrounded the figure of a *kachina*, a representation of a spirit being. With each step, he felt his energy increase. Suddenly he was overwhelmed with a vibration of love so deep it was as if someone flipped a switch within his heart. He looked over to Zoey, Cora, and Keri and saw the geometric figures in their energy field flare up in intensity as their energetic vibrations also increased.

"What's going on?" Zoey whispered. "My heart feels as though someone has covered it with a huge, fuzzy blanket."

"We seem to be drawn to places where some sort of prayer has taken place. These sacred sites and objects are increasing our vibration. We are experiencing energy, not from people, but from these sacred places." He paused, then looked at Zoey. "Are you seeing these symbols in our energy field?"

Zoey nodded. "I've never seen anything like them. What are these symbols?"

Alex took his time answering. When he finally did, he shook his head. "I don't know yet. But I do know these symbols are important to our timeline."

STAYING *in the* MOMENT

How many opportunities in life do you miss out on because you shut down, or don't stay present in the moment? You don't take the opportunity to learn from it, nor do you manifest what the possibilities of the moment could be if you hide from it. It's so easy to take your own perspective of fear or need to control to feel safe. But what is safety?

In the bigger picture of energy, the lesson is to be present and learn what you can from any given moment. Fear amplifies fear. That fear comes from something learned in your past. Yet think about this. Why would you want to project your past into your future? Consider those people you know, or it could even be yourself, who go through serial relationships because they can't let go of the past. They project their past into their present and future. They compound their fear with more fear and it makes everyone, including themselves, get stuck in that energy.

If you want to get off the merry-go-round, try to be energetically courageous to what the moment is trying to teach you. The lesson learned will allow you to move forward more openly into whatever your future holds.

Surrendering to the Experience

THAT NIGHT, despite the energy highs of the day, Alex felt exhausted. He sat on the edge of his hotel bed, trying to figure out why he felt as though he had some kind of hangover. He smiled as a thought popped into his head.

I must be experiencing an energy hangover. But what exactly does that mean?

He thought back over the events of that day. Their experiences at both the kiva and the sand paintings had been incredible. He'd reached heights of energetic vibrations he'd never reached before.

Maybe that was the issue.

His spiritual body was able to easily handle the higher vibrations. But his physical body, made up of much denser material, needed time to catch up to the higher energetic vibration. It made sense to him as he continued to think about, not only that day, but his life in general. When he'd gone to nature, mountains, these amazing sacred sites, his energy had increased. With that increase came the ability to see the geometric figures and colors around people. Could there really be a theme running through all of this? Were these symbols and colors always there, but because of where Alex had been energetically, he hadn't been able to see them until his energy increased exponentially?

Putting the pieces together, he realized that his energy experiences had something to do with attaining knowledge. What that knowledge was remained to be seen.

I'm too tired and overwhelmed by this heaviness to figure it out right now. I just want to sleep.

He crawled under the sheets and almost as soon as he hit the pillow he was fast asleep. Immediately, he dreamed he was standing amidst a magnificent mountain range. Everywhere he looked he saw high, snow-covered peaks and crags under a brilliant blue sky. It reminded him of pictures he'd seen of the Himalayas. In front of him he saw a sparkling white staircase leading up to what appeared to be a gold temple bathed in dazzling light. Each step was a different color. The first step was red, the second was orange, and so on.

It's the colors of the rainbow, he noticed.

He felt a swoosh of energy and when he looked down at his feet; he saw he was halfway up the staircase on a stair of yellow light. He couldn't explain it, but he had a knowing that somewhere, somehow, he'd climbed this staircase, stopping on the step he was on now. Was it possible this staircase had something to do with his energy hangover?

Looking back over his shoulder, he saw groups of people milling about on the first and second steps. They didn't appear to be able to move off the step they were on. The people on the first step—the red step—were hungry and in complete fear over their survival. They cried that they didn't want to die. The people on the second step were emotional and dramatic. He could hear them complaining that they couldn't keep climbing. It was impossible. They couldn't do it. Their feelings of sadness and despair were too powerful to overcome.

What did this all mean?

He felt the energies of the peoples on the first and second steps pulling at him, tugging him towards them, almost toppling him off the third step.

Wait a minute. The answer is staring me in the face. This whole staircase is about the choices we make in our lives. I'm no longer on the first step because I'm not in survival mode anymore. I don't fear whether I'll have enough money or a roof over my head. I've learned to trust that I will and it's worked out for me. I'm not on the second step because I've gone through all the emotional drama as an empath and learned how to be good with the energy and not get sucked into all of that. Learning those lessons has allowed me to walk up further on this staircase. I'm now standing on the yellow step. The place of will. What are the lessons of this step?

Alex awoke, his mind racing with the implications of his dream. His body still felt incredibly heavy and dense so obviously there was something he wasn't quite grasping. What piece of this puzzle was he missing?

He forced himself out of bed and padded across the room to get a drink of water. As he stood in the darkened room, he looked down and gasped when he saw the energy around him had taken on a yellow hue.

Now what the hell did that mean?

Confused and still suffering from his energy hangover, Alex finished his glass of water and went back to bed. He fell asleep and once again found himself confronted with his old friend, the white-robed man sitting atop the wall.

"Are you ready to listen yet?" the old man asked him.

"At this stage, what does listening mean?"

"As an empath, you should know that more than anybody. It means that you're listening to the energy."

"I am?"

"Yes. When you pay attention to the energy you're feeling in any given moment, you're actually listening to the energy. What has that taught you? What have the elements taught you?"

"Well, by listening, as you say, to the energy, I actually learned a lot from the experience. I didn't shut myself off or hide away as I'd done in the past. I just listened to the experience, had the experience, and discovered there's a bigger way."

The man nodded. "And do you know what that bigger way is?"

Alex thought about that for a long while. When the answer dawned on him, he was amazed at its simplicity. "The bigger way is that I have a choice."

"Yes you do. Everyone does. Every single facet of your life, the very fact that you were on that plane, the very fact that the man sitting next to you had a meltdown, the very fact that the child was crying, the very fact that you had the parents you had, the musical career that didn't pan out but brought you to other truths—everything along the way was preparing you to listen. And now here you are."

"Which is where?"

"The next step on the staircase. The place where you learn to surrender your will to a higher teaching."

The light streamed in through the window as Alex awoke. He lay in bed mulling over his dream. By the time he got up to take his shower, he'd come to the realization that surrendering to the experience was part of the learning process. And part of that learning process was being on this timeline he'd been slowly becoming aware of on this trip. Obviously everything up to this point was supposed to happen in order to teach. He'd learned that whatever the lesson was, the only way to access it was to surrender. He couldn't dictate what any given moment would or wouldn't be. He simply needed to allow the moment to unfold. Even surrendering to his exhaustion and not fighting it was part of a choice. The exhaustion was gone and he felt refreshed.

I wonder what's going to happen today.

He showered and changed and stepped out of his room. As he did so, he saw Zoey leaving her room. They met up and proceeded down to the breakfast room to grab a bite to eat and wait for the others to catch up. Along the way, he explained his two dreams to the young woman.

"I like your description of an energetic hangover," Zoey chuckled as they got their coffees. "I was so tired I couldn't move. It makes sense that since we're accessing higher vibrations of energy, our physical bodies need time to catch up." She took a sip of her coffee and continued. "Have you figured out what the dreams were trying to tell you?"

"I don't have all the pieces yet. But I do know that in order to navigate this timeline, we need to surrender to it. The dream showed me that you're at a particular point in your timeline depending on the choices you've made throughout your life. If you choose not to learn the lessons presented to you, you stay in a certain point and don't move forward."

"So is that why people seem to keep attracting the same things over and over to themselves, be it toxic relationships, lousy jobs, etc.? It's as if they keep manifesting their fears with the elements over and over again."

"I believe so. They're not paying attention to what the energy of their choices is trying to teach them. They get stuck in a rut and don't move forward. But if you're trying to do what we're all trying to do, understanding energy, surrendering to the energy, and learning whatever that energy has to teach, you get to move along on your timeline."

"And if you don't move along on your timeline in this life…?"

Alex took a sip of his coffee. "You get to come back and give it another shot."

"So explain to me what this surrender thing is all about."

"Think about it. Remember when you tried all those years to write fiction, but the energy didn't work out, yet it led you to something else that was just as wonderful? Think about Cora wanting to go shopping the other day. She used the elements to manifest that. How did it make us all feel?"

"Like crap."

"Exactly. The energy didn't work, but she forced it upon us and we accepted it. We became part of her manifestation. We lost a whole day because of our choice to follow an energy that didn't feel right to us. Now, think about yesterday. We didn't try to manifest anything out of our own will. We followed the energy presented to us and look where it led us. We were brought to not one, but two amazing energetic experiences. Why? Because we surrendered to it. And as we learned the lesson of surrender, you and I saw those geometric figures."

"Have you figured out what those are yet?"

"No. But I do know this. It's a part of the system of what we're learning. When the ladies finish breakfast, I'd like to go back to the sand painting."

Later that morning found the group standing again before the sand painting. This time however, Alex felt nothing. He stared at the painted symbols, trying to remember what they stood for. He walked around the painting, willing the energetic experience to happen. Still, he felt nothing. Cora and Keri grew restless as Alex tried to force the experience, only to find that the only energy he was feeling was the restive energy of the group and the excited energy of the other tourists milling about. Sinking into doubt, he noticed his energy tanking. He glanced over to Zoey and saw her trying to force herself to get into the energetic zone they'd gotten into the day before. But nothing happened. He grew frustrated as he realized something was wrong.

"Let's go," he finally said.

They climbed into the van and sat there quietly, trying to figure out what had just happened. Their thoughts were interrupted when Cora leaned forward between the seats and said, "Well, that was a total waste. I could have stayed in bed a bit longer instead of standing around staring at a bunch of colored sand."

The energy immediately grew worse.

"Well, obviously, we can't make an experience happen," Alex admitted.

"Could it be because we insisted it be one thing or another?" Zoey asked. "Maybe it isn't what we thought it was."

With that thought in mind, Alex took out his cell phone and made a call. "Okay, we're all set. I had to make reservations."

"Where are we going?" Keri asked.

"You'll see. It's an awesome spot with the most amazing petroglyphs."

He put the van in gear and they drove out into the desert. About an hour later, they pulled into a parking lot that was filled with cars. Alex turned the van off and sat quietly for a moment. "I'm feeling a bunch of stuff, but I think the energy is from all the tourists who have been here and are here now. Let's get out of the van and walk around. Try to just settle into the energy and see where it takes you."

The group poured out of the van. Alex felt a pull in a certain direction and started towards a large group of boulders. He looked about, but saw nothing that caught his attention. He was about to turn away when he felt that pull again. It was directing him towards the boulders. Shrugging his shoulders and practicing surrender, he walked up to the boulders. He stared at them, then on a hunch, walked behind them. Before him was a petroglyph of a man carved into the stone. As soon as he saw it, he felt his energy start to increase.

Here we go again.

As his energy increased, he watched the energy around the petroglyph begin to change according to how his own energy was changing. His vibration increased and he saw in his mind's eye the petroglyph being carved and the intention the carver put behind his work. It was the same feeling he'd had at the kiva.

His heart and throat opened. He felt his body releasing the tension from the experience at the sand painting. He felt as though he could step out of his physical body and fly away. What was going on?

Then it hit him.

Oh my God. The symbols aren't giving me energy. It's my own energy going through the symbols! The higher my frequency gets as I surrender to this experience and not dictate what it needs to be, there's some kind of knowledge being awakened in my physical body.

The tension was now completely gone. The heaviness and energy hangover was completely gone. He saw the colors of the rainbow beaming about him. It was all too incredible for words.

"Hey, we thought we'd lost you. What are you doing over here?"

Keri's voice abruptly brought him out of the experience. But he wasn't angry at the interruption. How could he be? He'd just learned something amazing.

"I just went through the coolest experience that helped me understand what happened at the sand painting."

By this time Zoey and Cora joined him and they sat down in the sand. "When we went back to the sand painting a second time, we expected to have the same energetic experience as we did yesterday. That's where we screwed up. We went back with the idea of making it happen from what we believed the symbols meant. It was almost as though I was pushing myself and my preconceptions on to the experience. Here, however, I got drawn into the experience, not knowing what it was going to be about. As I surrendered into what the experience could be, everything changed. My surrender allowed me to experience these symbols aligning with me."

"I'm not sure I get that," Cora responded.

"Surrender seems to be a key. Therefore, I'm going to continue to surrender to this whole process. Everything I've been through has taught me so many things, and the more I surrender my will into any given situation without trying to fight it or label it the way I think it should be, I'm allowed to see bigger and better things. Now these symbols are starting to serve some kind of purpose."

ACCESSING HIGHER TRUTHS

We lose so many opportunities to learn higher truths of what things can be. We always try to dictate. In our cleverness in what we have learned in our own knowledge, we always say this is one way or another.

This isn't so.

There are energetic opportunities where we can have higher truths come to us by not dictating from where we have come from in the past. As intellectual, sentient beings, we can sit, listen, think, and try to understand and develop new things and new experiences scientifically. However, maybe there's an energy within us that science will never understand until scientists, only using logic, finally surrender to it and allow it to be rather than dictate what they need it to be to fit their limited parameters. This is where opportunities are beginning to happen to many in this world. They are surrendering to the energetic experience without trying to make it fit into their parameters of logic. By doing this, they are allowing these symbols to filter through and have us align to them. It is as if we are remembering something that is already there within us, driving us forward in a quest to understand. But if we continue to dictate what these opportunities need to be, are we dictating that these truths are too deep for our limited minds to perceive?

Paying Attention to the Energy

IF THERE WAS ONE THING Alex learned over the years about energy work, it was that it always made him hungry. Yet, he didn't want to spoil the energetic high he was on by eating unhealthy food. They looked at their travel books and the GPS system in the van and found a restaurant that featured hearty salads on the menu.

As Alex drove towards the restaurant, he was excited. He was beginning to notice a theme to this trip they were on. No matter how low or high the energy became, as an empath who'd been subjected to feeling this all his life, he'd learned not to play into the emotions around him. By surrendering and allowing the energy to move through him without impediments (which usually consisted of him trying to label the energy a certain way), he was better able to navigate this timeline they were all on. All his teachings, all his experiences were demonstrating that this energy stuff was real. It wasn't easy to sit back and surrender—society dictated that people take charge of their lives and move ahead no matter what. But Alex was experiencing just the opposite. If he ran forward with his focus on taking charge, he'd miss listening to the energy. He'd miss the opportunity to make a choice in any given moment. He would definitely miss whatever the moment was trying to teach him, allowing him to learn it and move forward on his timeline. What he was doing may have been contrary to popular belief but, as he'd seen with the energy experiences at the kiva, the sand painting, and the petroglyph, he was receiving from a source that could not be seen or touched within humanity's limited perception of reality, that which others crave and only get from each other.

Reaching the restaurant, Alex noticed that it wasn't quite what he'd expected. It was huge and noisy and filled to capacity with people laughing too loud, yelling, and drinking a bit too much. The group was seated near the bar, which Alex immediately recognized was more of a pick-up place than an area to enjoy a quiet drink.

The waitress came up to their table and it was obvious by the look on her face and the tone of her voice that she was frazzled and frustrated. Alex felt himself losing his energetic objectivity as he unwittingly plugged into the crazy energies around him. As a result, he began to feel heavier and heavier.

Why is it that I can feel so light in these sacred places we've been visiting, yet I'm not in this place more than five minutes and I feel as though I want to throw up?

He fought to unplug from the various dramas swirling around him. He used the water element to move the energy through him and he felt the energy slowly ground out. His energy began to rise and soon he was seeing the colors of the people surrounding him. Many were muddy, though there were a few here and there whose colors were brighter. They were the ones sitting quietly by themselves or with a spouse, ignoring what was going on around them.

Taking this all in, Alex once more realized that the colors he was seeing reflected where the person was energetically. The waitress's color was dull because she was in an angry mood. Both the man at the bar and the blonde woman he was trying to pick up reflected muddy colors as he tried to get her sexual energy and she resisted.

Maybe that's why the sacred sites have such a higher vibration. When the ancient people did something sacred, they were surrendering to the sacred moment. Their only intention was to honor and respect. Those intentions are reflected in the energies they left behind and that we, as empaths, felt.

A light bulb went off in his head. Was this what the symbols were trying to teach him?

He was becoming overloaded again as his mind raced with possibilities. He needed to put this all aside and eat. They ordered their salads. When it was brought out to them, the salad looked fresh and tasty, but to Alex, something didn't feel quite right. Whatever he'd gone through back at the petroglyphs actually took him above the energy of the food. It was a weird feeling being torn this way, between the need to nourish himself and the need to just push the food away because spiritually he didn't need it.

However, his physical body did need nourishment and he began to eat. As he did so, he found his body grounding quicker, helping him come back to a place where he felt more in control of his feelings and emotions.

"You look out of sorts, my friend," Zoey spoke up. "What's going on?"

Alex took a sip of his iced tea. "It's been a strange, but interesting trip so far, hasn't it?"

"And we're not even halfway through with it yet!" Cora exclaimed.

"One thing I've learned from the experiences we've been having is to really pay attention to the energy. Being an empath, I've no choice, really."

"I know," Keri replied. "It's at times like this, in this room with all this crazy energy, that I find I struggle with my empathy. I just wish I didn't feel all that's going on around me."

"It is irritating," Alex concurred. "But if you don't judge it and just stay okay with it, it will move through you. By you judging it as crazy, it's sticking to you like glue."

"You make it sound so easy."

"That's because it is, once you break it down. Okay, let's take the Element of Air. All this shouting and loud laughing is getting on your nerves. The element of fire at the bar doesn't feel very good. We're not the only ones irritated in here; others' emotions are getting poked at. All of that is adding to a huge ball of gunk that can only be moved by the water element. The earth energy will then help you ground all these emotions you're feeling. Yet this trip is teaching me that something more is going on. It's as if by these energetic experiences, we're learning to rise above the elements—to rise above the physical reality of everyday life."

"What? We're learning to be those kinds of guys who meditate in a cave their whole life?" Cora asked.

"Far from it. The only way we've gotten even this far is because of everything we've been through already in our lives."

"What do you mean?"

"I wouldn't know that words can cut like a knife if I hadn't lived through it. At first I wanted to hide, but I learned to be present and navigate those emotions by surrendering and not judging. In my empathic experiences, there were moments I was overloaded. It didn't feel good. Whenever I tried to dictate what it should be, it got worse. Look at what we went through at the sand painting. Something magical happened that got my attention. We loved it so much we went back and tried to make it happen again. But it didn't happen. It's as if its energetic lesson was already gifted and learned. We found the petroglyphs and it happened again. Why? Because we didn't force it." He paused as he looked to each one of his companions. "Here's a thought to chew on. How many things in your life do you think were placed there on your path to show you an experience that many people don't get to have simply because they think it has to be a certain way? They dictate the outcome from a place of their will. How many times do we keep going back, trying to relive moments, trying to re-create that perfect 'Norman Rockwell' moment, only to be disappointed in a lesser than or no feeling experience?"

"That's a lot to think about," Keri murmured.

"It's not that we're special or better than anybody else. Everyone in this restaurant has had the same opportunities we've had. The difference is that we've paid attention. Consider this. Everything we've been going through our entire lives as empaths, including this trip, has been about feeling. As we became okay with that feeling, we learned to navigate and surrender to it. And what happened? These profound knowings, even beyond our physical experience, are starting to make themselves present. We wouldn't have gotten here without all that other stuff. Maybe along the way, there was some kind of map. Some kind of process. This timeline they keep showing us. But on the timeline, as we all know, some things have happened that were not pleasant. Everyone goes through that. In those moments, we have a choice. Those of us who become fearful or get trapped into victimhood go another path and seem to get stuck in a perpetual merry-go-round of the same drama over and over again. For whatever reason, we've discovered there's got to be more. So in our energetic curiosity and courage, we've continued to surrender to the next thing along the way. Each time we do that, we have an experience that builds upon the last experience. It reminds me of the dream I had—the staircase with colors. I'm looking around at these people here and seeing their colors and you know what? Their colors are dingy, washed out. Why? Because like the people I saw at the bottom of the staircase, their lesson is to be okay with who they are. Everyone in this room seems to be coming from where they believe they need to be coming from, instead of surrendering. They're dictating who they are in their experience. I think that's why their colors are dimmed. They're in a fight or flight mode of thinking. They aren't listening to the energy. When they finally make a choice, it's more reactive than proactive. Maybe they haven't reached the point I did where I got sick and tired of being sick and tired and realized there had to be something more to my life."

"What about these symbols? Do they mean anything?" Zoey asked.

"I'm beginning to believe these symbols were put in our timeline so that we as individuals have an opportunity to learn how to increase our ability to be okay in any moment. Maybe they're reminders of something bigger."

"And what would that something bigger be?"

"I'll be honest with you. As you know, I've had a lot of relationships in my life. Some that were fantastic and some that almost killed me. But I have never felt love from anybody as much as I felt in that kiva. Or looking at those petroglyphs and the sand painting. It was as though I transcended all the human explanations of what love is or should be and tapped into something more pure, more uncorrupted by human intention."

Cora frowned. "I didn't have the same experience as you."

"Why is that?"

"Well, I went into this whole trip with the thought that it was going to be some kind of vacation. We're just here to have fun with some energetic lessons thrown in."

Alex chuckled. "Well, I respect you for being honest. But our trip is bigger than even we at first imagined. Our timeline doesn't seem to want us to get tripped up by ego and pushing our will on each other. The timeline wants us to experience these places we've been going to, the spaces we're experiencing and the symbols we're seeing to show us the next step or vibration or feeling in our bodies. And look where it's led us. Cora, if you just let go of what you think this trip has to be and just be present to whatever we experience, I'm sure you'll feel all that I'm feeling. Maybe even more." Alex spread his hands on the table and looked at his companions. "This whole trip so far has gotten my attention. I'm hooked to see what the next energetic moment brings."

"What is the point of all this though?" Cora continued. "Why are we boomeranging up and down with our energy? What purpose does all this serve?"

"If you think about it, there's a goal here somewhere. And the goal, if I go by my dream, is the top of those stairs. Maybe part of the goal is as simple as having these energy experiences and growing higher and higher in vibration in order to see more symbols. I don't know how they interact; all I know is that when I get to a space where they're the same color I'm projecting, they change me. It's turning out that this curse of empathy is starting to look like the greatest gift we could ever imagine."

"Are you nuts?" Keri asked incredulously.

Alex laughed. "It does sound nutty, doesn't it? Empaths constantly have to feel all this energetic crap. We're constantly getting beaten up energetically and we feel as though we're constantly suffering. But think about what you experienced today. That love I felt at the kiva has no words that could adequately describe it. Those situations where we actually transcended time and felt the timelines of the ancient peoples wouldn't have happened if we hadn't gone through all those years of suffering. It really does get to a point where you can't hide away anymore. You want to understand why you are the way you are and what that means. Five years ago, none of what we've been through so far on this trip would have happened. Two years ago, two weeks ago. But it happened because we were ready. And we'll be ready for whatever else is presented to us."

"So what are we doing tomorrow?"

"Let's get everyone engaged in this and sleep on it. We'll get up in the morning and have a goal. Not so much a goal that tells us we have to be here or there. Rather a goal that says we're open to any and all experiences and we'll see if something pops up. If there is a plan to this whole trip, maybe the important thing at this moment is to figure out how to access this plan. Obviously our brains and needs aren't helping any, and our fears or guilt or empathic ability or even our skill to manifest with the elements isn't helping any. Let's open up to the possibility that there's another truth for us as a group as to why we're here."

Deciding it was time to just sit back and enjoy themselves, the group began to swap stories and laugh and have a good time. After about fifteen minutes of laughing hysterically at some of the stories that were being shared, Alex held up his hand. "Hey, stop for a minute. Have you noticed how good you feel? How much lighter your energy is?" The ladies looked at each other and nodded. "I think we're on the plan right now, even talking about it. We're looking at higher things. Feel how you feel right now. Now look around you. Doesn't it feel as though the bar has calmed down? And look at our waitress. Why, she's smiling! There's a clue in that."

THE GIFT *of* PAYING ATTENTION

Many times we forget there's a subtlety to what we feel—those moments in the woods or sitting on a beach where we feel wonderful. It's sad that with our hectic lifestyles, many don't even realize they're feeling. They don't pay attention to the energy of their feelings. They brush their feelings and emotions aside in an effort to get to the next meeting, to reach a crying child, to buy the next toy. They're still at the beginning of their life lessons of not paying attention to the emotions they're having—the crankiness or uncomfortability they're feeling in their bodies. Could all these things be happening in an effort to get our attention to shift us up just a little to have a bigger understanding of what this world is trying to teach us? As we control and dictate from a place of what we believe is right or wrong, good or evil, that subtle opportunity to feel and just know there's a bigger picture is lost. What if we paid attention to the energies of our manifestations we put out into the world and into each other? Is it possible that by doing that, we can begin to see there's another way of being? One of less control and more trust that there truly is a method to the madness?

Energetic Integrity

THE NEXT DAY the skies were gray and overcast. Yet Alex was in an adventurous mood. So much had happened in such a short period of time. It whetted his curiosity to see what this day would bring.

Sitting around the breakfast table, Cora asked, "You were talking about the timeline yesterday. Who makes this timeline anyway?"

Alex said, "I think the timeline has always been there. There was a timeline of those people in the kiva. There was a timeline of the man who carved the petroglyphs. There's a timeline of us. We don't know why, but here we are in Arizona learning all this crazy stuff. There's the timeline of the man on the plane. Right in that moment he had to be sitting next to me."

"People might call that coincidence," Keri said.

"If you believe in this timeline, there really are no coincidences. Look at you, for example. You were on your way to get your nails done when you passed by a shop where I was teaching a class on empathy. Something told you to cancel your nail appointment and come to the class. Was that a coincidence?"

"The way you describe it, I guess it wasn't."

"The timeline pulled you to make a choice that day. Nails or class. You chose class. And it's changed your way of thinking, hasn't it?"

"Yes it has." Keri paused, then continued. "But what would have happened if I hadn't chosen to cancel my nail appointment that day?"

"I believe that if it was on your timeline to meet me, it would have happened eventually. Maybe not on that day, but at another location, at another time."

"Are you trying to tell me our entire life is pre-ordained? That we really have no choices?"

"No. We do have choices. What I'm beginning to understand, however, is that our choices come down to when something will happen. We've all come to believe that our life is a series of lessons to be learned. Those lessons and opportunities are on our timeline. However, if we choose not to learn them, they continue to pop up in our lives until we finally choose to learn them."

"So it doesn't necessarily mean we'll learn them in this lifetime?"

"Correct." Alex turned to Zoey. "You didn't have the money to come on this trip. But just a few weeks before we were going to leave, your boss called you into his office and asked you to work overtime on a project which gave you the money to come. Coincidence?"

Zoey shook her head. "Nope. It was part of this timeline you're talking about. Even though I could have chosen to take that money and buy something else with it, I had a knowing that I'd been given the opportunity to earn that money because I needed to go on this trip."

"Exactly."

After paying their bill, they were headed towards their van when they passed an old woman dressed in patched clothing. She was short and plump with a round, deeply tanned face. The corners of her eyes were crinkled with the years she'd lived, but there was a sweet smile on her face as she beckoned them towards her small fruit stand she'd set up in the corner of the parking lot. The group strode over and ended up buying enough fruit to get them through the next few days.

"What a nice lady," Keri replied, waving to the woman as they drove past.

"What else did her energy tell you?" Alex prompted.

Keri thought about it for a moment. "Well, it's obvious she doesn't have much in the way of possessions or even clothing. But you know, she was happy. Her energy made me feel good."

"Good observation. She was okay with who she was and where she is in her life. Yeah, it could be better. But she's made her peace with it. Contrast that to the man on the plane. He had more money than that woman will ever see, but his energy was awful. He was definitely not someone you would call happy. So obviously money doesn't seem to be part of the solution to have good energy."

"Not all people who are poor are happy like that woman," Cora pointed out.

"Money as a focus isn't what brings you happiness. Amassing a lot of things doesn't always bring you happiness. However, what if you were happy with the things you have, or where you are in life? Look at me. I live in a tiny house that's maybe 900 square feet. I don't have the marble countertops or the jetted tub or crown molding all throughout my living room. But I'm happy. I'm content with what I have. I experience being okay in any given moment and it makes that moment perfect. And if I'm supposed to live in a larger house that has that jetted tub and marble countertops, then so be it. The Universe will find a way to help me get those things. The point is, I'll be okay no matter what."

Alex felt the energy shift. Glancing in the rearview mirror, he saw Cora seated in the back seat of the van with a frown on her face.

"Why does what I say bother you?" he asked gently.

"Because I have all that stuff you're talking about. I live in a huge house with the Carrera marble and jetted tub and the whole nine yards. Yet, sitting here, I realize I'm not happy. Not like you. All that stuff is nice, but my husband and I have to work hard to keep it up. Higher taxes, more maintenance, more time spent keeping it all clean."

Alex smiled. "I do have more time to spend on my timeline because I don't have the burden you do to maintain all that. You see, if I go into a space of being okay with what I have, I'm not worried. If I'm worried, I'm not sending out a good vibe. Anyone who is sensitive to energies won't want to be around me because of the bad vibe I'm sending out. If I'm selling a product and my energy is lousy, people may not want to buy from me. But if I'm in a space of okay, they'll want to be around me, or buy my products because my energy makes them feel good. Then I'll be more abundant if that's what my timeline dictates."

"And why wouldn't your timeline dictate abundance?"

"Abundance doesn't always mean having lots of money or material things. Abundance is also peace of mind and being okay with where I am in the world. I believe I've learned the lessons the timeline had for me about being so focused on money because even though I might be considered not so well off because I don't live in a mansion, I'm fine with where I am and more importantly with who I am. I know there are more lessons on my timeline. Heck, this whole trip so far has been one lesson after another. But I'm okay with that. In fact, I look forward to seeing what the next lesson is."

"I've learned the things that are in my life physically are more of a tool than something I need to get energy from. It's almost as if the things I'm getting or aligning to me on my timeline are things I've manifested that I need to propel me to the next part of my timeline. They're not something that keeps me stuck. If I needed a big mansion, it would be part of my timeline to do something to own it. But if I get that mansion and I'm working my butt off to keep it going, or I get it to get attention from others by having them ooh and aah about how wonderful I am, how would that really make me feel better? How would that help me achieve a higher truth about who I am and what my life is all about? I would just be getting people energy. And as we've learned both on the plane and in the restaurant, people energy isn't always the best. What I really want are the things I need to manifest to move me forward on my timeline."

He could see Cora mulling over his words. A few moments passed before she asked, "How do you explain violence? Is that also part of a timeline?"

"Let me tell you a story. It's starting to make sense to me now, though it didn't at the time. About fifteen years ago, I was living in a tiny apartment between bands. I couldn't afford much, just my guitar and a portable recorder that I worked hard to buy. I loved that recorder. One of my friends called and asked if I wanted to record. I said yeah, but my car wasn't working. My friend said I'll come get you. Meet me in the center of downtown. He got off the phone, and since we weren't meeting for a few hours, I lay down and fell asleep. I had a dream in which a group of gang members were walking towards me up a hill. It was so real that when I woke up, I went immediately into fear. It didn't help when it dawned on me that I was meeting my friend in the center of downtown, which was in a very dicey neighborhood. My first thought was, 'Crap. I'll be carrying my guitar and recorder. Perfect things to steal from me. I went right into instant fear and panic. My energy tanked. I couldn't call my friend back because I was so consumed with fear, it screwed up my energy and I couldn't even remember his number. I had no choice but to suck it up and take my chances. Walking down the street with guitar and recorder, I heard a dog barking. I didn't think anything of it. Suddenly, looking down the hill, I saw a gang walking towards me. Oh no! My dream must have been a warning. I kept asking myself, what do I do now? All of a sudden, I heard the dog bark again. Thank God I paid attention to that dog barking, because there was the answer to my question. I realized dogs smell fear. I needed to change my energy and get out of fear. I got into a space of being okay. The gang came up to me, greeted me, and kept going. It was as if they didn't even see my guitar and recorder. The moral of the story is that empathic people always complain about what they feel from other people. But the question you should ask is, what are people feeling from me?"

"But that still doesn't explain all the violence in the world."

"Okay. Think back to the other day when you wanted to go shopping. It didn't feel good and we got sucked into it and off we went. It didn't turn out so great. Now look at that from a bigger perspective. Here we are having these experiences of these geometric symbols and shapes. When we're in a really good space and our energy gets high, it's almost as though the energy mirrors back through us this wonderful experience. The only way we can get there is by surrendering to the thought that maybe it doesn't mean what we think it means. But how much of that is in the world? So many people in the world are in a strong fearful place of control, where they dictate what the symbols and the teaching in their lives mean. They get others ingrained in that same thought process. All of a sudden you have 5 people, 10 people, 100 people all feeling unempowered. Mired in victimhood. Unvalidated. Not being able to manifest what they want. They crave validation for their point of view and will stop at nothing, including committing acts of unspeakable violence, to get the validation they need for whatever thought process they're trying to perpetuate. Now you have a big energy ball of yuck. That's hard to climb out of. Not to pick on you, Cora, but you created a community manifestation by pushing your manifestation on to the group. We bought into it to keep the peace. Many people buy into community manifestation because they believe, or more importantly, want to believe what they're being told. They become trapped in the energy of being less than. Instead of listening to the purity of the energy in any given moment, they instead listen to the energy of someone else who enmeshes them in his own manifestation. They're always promised things will get better to draw them in deeper to the leaders' thoughts and manifestations. You'll be rich beyond measure, they're told. You'll never want for anything ever again. But when does that happen? Think of all the revolutions throughout history. The leaders succeeded in getting what they'd promised. What about the little guy? Did he really come out much better? It's as if they're all stuck on the lower end of that part of their timeline that teaches what you do with your own energy and your own manifestations without getting sucked into someone else's."

"So it really does come down to choice?" Zoey asked.

"Yes."

The group fell silent as they took in Alex's words.

A few miles down the road, they drove past a new age store that was having a sale on crystals. Alex was about to drive by when he felt that inexplicable pull to stop and go inside. "What do you say to exploring that store?" he asked the group.

"Sounds like a plan!" Zoey agreed.

He pulled into the parking spot in front of the shop and they piled out. Entering, they were assailed with the rich fragrance of incense wafting through the air. They found a large, well-maintained store with all sorts of crystals, sage, and other new age items in eye-catching displays. Cora and Keri immediately made their way towards the crystals. "These are gorgeous!" Cora cooed as she picked up a large quartz crystal. Keri joined her with a shopping basket. Unable to stop, they'd pick up a crystal, feel its energy, and immediately drop it into the shopping basket. It wasn't long before they were off grabbing another basket to excitedly fill with their purchases.

Meanwhile, Alex slowly strolled throughout the store, randomly picking up crystals here and there, feeling them in his hand, before replacing them and moving on. At the back of the store, he paused in front of posters and paintings of the chakra system and the geometric figures painted within each chakra. He was studying the figures when Zoey sidled up next to him.

"Did you see the prices of these crystals that are supposed to be on sale?" she whispered. He shook his head. "I was so drawn to some of them, but as soon as I looked at the price tag, I almost died. They're asking $400 for a medium-sized piece of rose quartz. $500 for a quartz crystal."

Alex's eyes widened. "Are you kidding me? We can get those at home for a quarter of the price."

"I know!"

Alex turned and headed towards a table where polished pieces of selenite, amber, celestite, and other crystals were carefully laid out. He picked up a piece of selenite and held it in his hand. He frowned as he handed the selenite to Zoey. "Hold that and tell me what you feel."

Zoey wrapped her fingers around the cool mineral. She immediately felt a heaviness in the pit of her stomach. "It feels awful," she concluded.

"Precisely."

"I've held selenite countless times. It's never felt as nasty as that piece. Why is that?"

"Among other properties, selenite is a stone of honesty and truth." He grabbed the celestite and handed it to her. "Try holding that one and tell me what you feel."

She wrapped her fingers around the sky blue stone and once again felt her stomach tighten. "That one feels awful too. Yet I know celestite helps you communicate with the angelic realm so its vibration should be pretty high."

"Keep holding the stone while you close your eyes. Tell me if you see anything."

Zoey did as he asked. She remained standing quietly with her eyes closed. It wasn't long before her brow furrowed with bewilderment. "That's weird. I'm seeing a woman with long blonde hair that comes down to her waist." She quickly picked up the selenite and closed her eyes. "Okay, this is beyond weird now. I'm seeing her again with this stone. As I focus on her, my stomach gets even tighter."

"Same thing happened to me."

"Who is she?"

"I'm not sure."

Zoey replaced the stones and noticed Cora and Keri running about the store, excitedly shoving crystals into their shopping basket. "Look at them. They're going to spend all the money they brought and then some on all those stones."

They watched as their two companions finally called a halt to their shopping spree. Just as they approached the cash register, a door opened behind the counter and a woman stepped out. Zoey gasped. "Oh my God! That's the woman I saw while holding those crystals."

"I thought as much."

She looked up at Alex. "You figured this out, didn't you?"

"I believe so. My guess is that woman is the owner of this store. And I bet you, she put her thoughts and feelings and energies into all these stones."

"Are you kidding me? Are you telling me she put the energy of 'you need to buy this' into her merchandise? Any sensitive person who doesn't know the difference would follow that energy and buy all this overpriced stuff. Jeez, that's insidious!"

"It happens more often than you think."

"Should we say something to Cora and Keri? They're not going to appreciate being taken advantage of like that," Zoey asked.

"No. There's a reason I was drawn to come in here. I have a feeling there's a lesson here that we need to pay attention to. How often have you watched commercials on TV or magazines that tell you that in order to fit in, you need to buy their product? It's all part of that community manifestation we experienced when Cora wanted to go shopping. We all got sucked into doing what she wanted to do. In the end, she just wanted to spend money, to buy things. This is the same, but it's slightly different lesson, not only for Cora and Keri, but for us as well."

Unwilling to stand any longer in the lousy energy she was feeling, Zoey walked out of the store. A few moments later, Alex joined her. He immediately felt her agitation.

"I get what you're saying," Zoey exclaimed angrily. "I know there's a lesson in here for all of us. But I can't move past what that woman did. It just ticks me off. I want so badly to go back into that store and say something to that woman and let her know that we're on to her dirty trick."

"Why?"

"Because what she's doing is so wrong! It's—it's energetic integrity abuse!"

Alex laughed. "That's a good way to put it."

"I don't like that my friends are getting so bamboozled. Lesson or no lesson, I am going to say something to that woman!"

She turned on her heel and swung open the door.

CHOICES

The bad stuff in the world is all choice. Consider these two possibilities. In the stories above, the energy in the restaurant and the bar didn't feel too good at first. As the energies of Alex and his friends got better, it seemed as though the place calmed down. Maybe the job of an empath is to really learn how to get into a good space energetically. When they start to feel good, that begins to transmute or change the energy around them. It works much like a tree changing carbon dioxide into oxygen. Perhaps empaths should take a clue from that. But if an empath is sitting in a place of fear or disgust, they're only adding their own emotions of fear and disgust to the malaise around them. The second possibility is that when something does happen, what kind of energetic choice do we make? As empaths, we've learned from the elements how to navigate and surrender. When things happen in a person's life, and they become fearful, they're putting that out into the world. Yet in reality, when things go awry, they have a choice. Do they become victim to that energetic moment and add to the swamp of fear and yucky energy, or do they rise above it and see it as a teacher on their timeline?

Lessons of the Geometry

ALEX FELT ZOEY'S ANGER as a ball in the pit of his own stomach. Knowing how easily her temper could spiral, and wanting to avoid a confrontation with the store owner, he reached out and pulled her back. "Wait just a second. Take a deep breath. You yelling at that woman isn't going to accomplish anything. In fact, you'll be interfering in Cora and Keri's lesson." That slowed Zoey's step. She allowed Alex to lead her back to the van. He opened the door and they sat inside.

"Let's look at this whole situation from an energetic point of view. How does your energy feel right now?"

"It feels like crap," she admitted.

"Yes it does. Do you know why?"

"Because I wanted to scream at that woman?"

"Because you wanting to scream at her means you judged her."

"How could I not judge her? What she's doing is unethical!"

"I understand that, Zoey. But remember what we're trying to do here. We're trying to listen to the energies around us and learn from them."

Zoey took a deep breath to steady herself. "Okay, you're right."

"If you look at what happened from a different point of view, she's really doing what animals do in nature. They use camouflage to fake out their prey. Is that really any different from what she did? She's using camouflage to get people to buy things they really don't need. It's what keeps her in business. Yet, looking at the bigger picture here, how is that woman supposed to be? How are we all supposed to be? Maybe there's an opportunity for some kind of evolution to take place here. To go from a place where someone has to do what that woman did to gather money to herself because they don't have trust or enough faith that abundance is there, to getting to a space where they know and accept that it's there. Her mistrust about abundance caused her to put that energy on her products. That tells me she's stuck in that part of her timeline where that lesson is. She's stagnating. She's not moving ahead."

"Now that I think of it, the whole energy of the store felt stagnant," Zoey agreed.

"Exactly. Her thoughts and energies are going against the flow of energetic integrity and trust."

"How does that play into the timeline?"

"It goes back to evolution. We're starting to see something here. We both feel really heavy right now. You plugged into her and I plugged into you. Maybe the whole thought process of the timeline is learning how it moves forward."

"Okay," Zoey said. "So how do we actually get to the next place?"

"Let's break this down. We went into the store feeling pretty good, and we were given an experience. We picked up the crystals and had a realization of what was happening energetically. Yet, we judged and our energy tanked while Cora and Keri are still in there, gleefully buying up the store."

"Why is that?"

Alex sat back in his seat and looked out the windshield at the surrounding desert. "They obviously had a different experience than we did. I think it has something to do with how far you are on that staircase I told you about. I have a funny feeling you and I went backwards on our timeline and got stuck, while Cora and Keri actually went forward on their timeline."

"We did?" Zoey asked incredulously.

"You and I have spent years doing some deep healing, overcoming issues, and learning so much about energy and how it works. Cora and Keri are still new to all of this. They don't feel as much as you and I do. I don't believe they're at the same point we are on our timelines. Yet our timelines all intersected at the same point, making sure we all went into that store. They became ecstatic over the crystals because they needed to feel that way to move on in their timeline. The crystals made them feel good. I guarantee you, they'll be questioning why they bought those crystals in the first place. But they wouldn't be asking that and learning about the energy put into those crystals if they hadn't experienced needing to buy them in the first place. Are you with me so far?"

Zoey nodded. "I think so. But how did they move on their timeline if they got sucked into that woman's manifestation?"

"Now we didn't need to buy the crystals. We just held them and felt the energy. And we discerned what the energy on the crystals was all about. Our mistake is that we judged that energy and it stopped us on our timeline. We didn't move forward. It was the choice we made in the moment. I'm beginning to understand that the timeline is a chance to make choices. We chose not to buy, but we chose to plug in and judge. Cora and Keri are following their timeline to buy something that makes them feel good. Sooner or later, they'll realize they don't need the crystals to make them feel good, or that no matter how much stuff they buy, the energy won't be enough. In other words, they needed to buy the crystals in order to learn that they didn't need to buy the crystals."

"Expensive lesson," Zoey said.

"Sometimes they are. Maybe those are the ones we really pay attention to. When we judged that woman, we took a step backwards on our timeline."

"So basically what you're telling me is that we really need to look at our judgments and realize that everyone has their own timelines designed to help teach. Just as we have our timeline, that woman in the store has hers. I have to be okay with where she is. I may not agree with it, but I can't judge her because she's at a different place from where I am." Zoey paused as she mulled this over. "It seems to me that when we judged, we got pulled down that staircase you told me you dreamed about."

Alex nodded. "Interesting. Guess we'll have to be more viligant on how to move forward and not backwards."

"At least the cool thing is that we're aware of it. We'll make mistakes because we're human. But when we do, we can quickly correct ourselves. But we need to keep aware that every time we judge, it's like an anchor around our ankles that, as you said, pulls us backwards on that staircase. Tell me, how does your energy feel now?"

"It's starting to get better. But I'd still like to get out into the desert and move the rest of the crummy energy off of me."

"Great idea. But don't forget. Our goal, as empaths, is to one day be able to stand in the middle of the yuckiest energy, no matter where it is and not get sucked into it. Our jobs are to transmute the energy, not add to it."

Zoey smiled. "I'm trying. I'm trying."

At that moment, Cora and Keri emerged from the store. They both held two bags each filled with crystals and other items they'd bought in the store.

"You should see the stuff we got! They're amazing!" Keri exclaimed as they piled their bags into the back of the van.

"That was an awesome store," Cora concurred. "Unfortunately, I spent most of my extra cash. We're really going to have to watch our pennies. We still have five days to go before we leave Arizona."

Alex and Zoey smiled as they glanced at each other.

"In honor of all the stones you bought, I say we head out to the Petrified Forest," Zoey replied. "I don't know why, but the name just popped into my head. I think we need to go there next."

"Hey, you just said that and the sun came out from behind the clouds," Keri noticed. "It's a sign!"

"It must be," Zoey chuckled as Alex put the van in gear and pulled out of the parking lot.

Although Alex felt the Petrified Forest was the next place to visit, he still felt a slight trepidation in his heart. He'd grown up feeling especially close to trees. They'd saved his sanity countless times as he ran to them for solace after a trying day attempting to navigate his life as an empathic child. He knew tree energy felt much better than people energy. But the Petrified Forest, though beautiful, was in reality a graveyard for dead trees that had fossilized into stone. What kind of vibration, if any, would these dead trees have? What if, instead of feeling the love and joy he usually felt when he around trees, he instead felt sad and depressed because they were dead?

Alex immediately shook himself out of that thought process.

If there's one thing I've learned over the years, it is not to judge a situation. I just need to be open and to surrender to the experience of going into the Petrified Forest. My only intention is to be open to feel whatever is there. And if there is nothing, so be it.

The ride was less than an hour.

The Petrified Forest National Park, located in northern Arizona, is a walk back through time in a place where dinosaurs once roamed over 225 million years ago. The area was once lush with green forests and tropical marshland. Then, in an instant they were gone when the volcanic mountains surrounding the area erupted, toppling the trees. Swept away by water and covered by volcanic ash and sediment, the trees became entombed. Over the next millions of years, the remains of the trees became petrified, turning their bark into stone. Erosion over the years slowly exposed the logs and remnant pieces of what were once majestic pines.

When the group arrived, they each went off on their own to explore. Zoey slowly made her way towards a large petrified trunk, her senses wide open to whatever experience was awaiting her. It didn't take long before a calmness came over her, helping the young woman to return to a space of balance.

Alex sat down near what had once been a huge conifer, now toppled and lying on its side. He couldn't quite believe what he was feeling. Although this tree had been dead for centuries, he could still feel its energy. Like Zoey, it didn't take long for him to start feeling calm and peaceful. He gently placed his hand on the petrified trunk and felt his heart open up. Energy poured into him, increasing his vibration.

Glancing to his left, he saw at the foot of the trunk a piece that had broken off. With signs everywhere prohibiting anyone from taking the petrified wood, he didn't dare pick it up. But he was in awe when he realized the piece was in the shape of a perfect heart. It wasn't jagged like the other pieces of petrified wood that were lying about. This piece was smooth. The more he studied the heart shaped stone, the more his own heart opened up.

What was going on? Was this a reminder? A trigger? For what? The answer came to him in a flash.

It's the geometry of the tree.

But what did that mean?

He pondered the statement as he looked about him, at the surrounding desert, at the birds flying in the sky. Looking down, he saw ants going about their business near his boot.

Could it be that everything has a geometry? It seemed to him that the geometry is what told the tree it was a tree. Just as the geometry told the ants they were ants and the birds were birds. He'd been seeing these figures off and on in people since arriving in Arizona. Was it possible that human geometry was the same as this tree's geometry?

He heard a distinct voice in his ear, whispering to him to "take my heart." He quickly looked about him, but he was alone. Once again he heard the whisper, "take my heart." He looked down at the heart-shaped petrified wood and started to reach for it. At that moment, a realization hit him, and he pulled his hand back.

The perfectly shaped heart had nothing to do with the petrified trunk.

It was a sign, a visual recognition to anyone who was open to the concept that right here, in this very moment, Alex's timeline and the petrified tree's timeline were intersecting. For whatever reason, he was supposed to be here, to experience and feel what he was feeling. His geometry and the geometry of the tree were meeting because both their energetic vibrations were becoming one and the same.

Alex was in awe as he felt his heart continue to open with the love that was pouring into him. Although the tree was supposedly dead, he knew this wasn't so. He felt its spirit. Its energy was shining through his geometry and he was feeling what it was like to be a tree. It was peaceful and wonderful and so accepting that this is what the tree was made for. It was made to stand tall in a forest and process carbon dioxide into oxygen. It was made to serve as homes for birds and insects. It was made to reproduce through its pine cones. It was happy being what it had been created for. Its geometry was those strange figures Alex had been seeing since arriving in Arizona. Its geometric figures are what allowed all this energy to come in freely. The energy was known by different names in every culture: the chi, the holy spirit, wind horse. It aligned through the geometry of the tree, unimpeded by fear, or by the desire to manifest something different or not be who it was.

As it shone through without all these blocks and lesser than energies, it also flowed out. A continual ebb and flow of energy. In that moment, all the lessons Alex had learned throughout his life, his own openness to whatever each moment had to teach or share with him, perfectly aligned to the geometry of the tree.

Alex felt humbled by this experience. Why couldn't people be the same as the tree? Why did they insist on mucking things up and making their lives much more complicated than they needed to be?

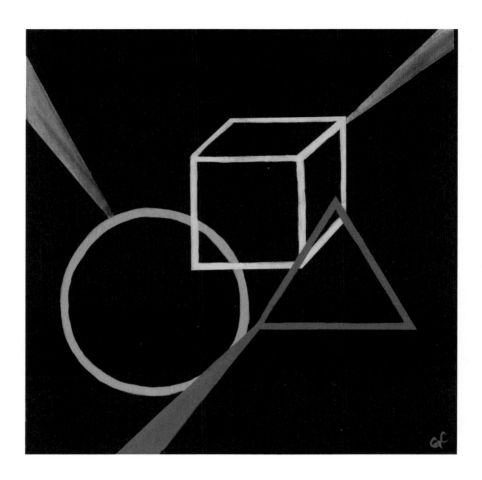

Alex pondered this. Although the tree still had a spirit, he believed it had finished its timeline. In so doing, it had arrived at the perfect geometric figure of the heart, which recognized that the tree had fulfilled its reason for being. It had achieved part of its destiny. Its continuing task was to wait for as long as it took for someone's timeline—someone who was open to its possibilities—to intersect with its own timeline and comprehend its teachings.

It had taken millions of years, but now even its task was continuing. There would be others who would make their way here and feel and try to comprehend this energy. Alex knew the gift he'd just been given, but he also knew his journey of understanding was still underway.

As he sat with the tree and felt its love continue to pour into him, he thought about the human race. It seemed to Alex that if people opened their eyes and got out of their own way, they would notice the constant reminders of what they had the potential to become on their timeline. It was becoming clear to him that these geometric figures had something to do with that.

Suddenly Alex felt what could only be described as a slight explosion of energy in his chest. He caught his breath as he felt its energy scatter throughout his body.

What the heck was that?

He looked down at his hands and saw tiny flickers of light coalesce around his fingertips before disappearing. It reminded him of fireworks when they fizzle out in dozens of tiny lights before vanishing.

Oh my God! I think I know what just happened!

His mind raced with possibilities. Was it possible that these figures held a person's lesson within its shape? He'd heard the term "sacred geometry" many times, but it was only now starting to make sense.

He thought back to the crystal shop they'd visited. These figures were in the posters depicting the chakras. He knew from experience that a person's issues lay within their chakra system. He could feel those issues in a person's energy field because of his empathic abilities. The chakras held the blocks or trauma an individual experienced throughout their life. For example, if a person felt unworthy, or not comfortable in their own skin, they needed to heal their first chakra. If someone never spoke their truth, they needed to heal their fifth chakra, and so on. He put his hand to his mouth as he realized the colors of the staircase in his dream corresponded to the chakra system. Those people he'd seen on the first and second steps were still in the midst of healing their first and second chakras. That was why they were still stuck on those steps. They'd hadn't healed those issues yet.

Depending on where a person was on their timeline determined how much light shone through whatever their lesson, represented by one of these figures, was at that moment. The question now was how did the vibration of his energy work with these geometries? Did they somehow work together? How?

He felt something brush his cheek. Pulling his head back, he saw what looked like a dandelion seed waft down and land on his knee. His first thought was—is this a geometry or it is energy?

He thought back to the petrified tree. It had an energy that shone through its geometry. Its geometry was its blueprint for being. Its breath of life shining through the life force that is in everything. He looked out over the desert and for the first time noticed the tiny flowers growing in what many would consider harsh, inhospitable land. Yet here on his lap was a seed. The beginnings of life. It was as if the geometry of this tiny seed sent it forth to find a space where it could land. Joining with the energy of the sun, a process began, the shell of the seed opened and it began its destiny of growing into a flower.

He turned his mind to this trip, to how much he'd changed since getting on the plane. Every time a higher vibration came to him, whether at the kiva or the sand painting or sitting here in the Petrified Forest, a thought or a knowing released that, like the tiny seed, sprouted new life within him—a new piece of knowledge that led him further along his timeline.

Maybe this is what life is all about. Maybe our lives are made up of a set of geometries along our timeline. When a person has an energetic moment of choice and they make that choice from a place of feeling the highest energetic truth, it takes them to a new place, a new life, a bigger and more complex life. Not from a place of lower energetic trouble or drama, but from a space where spiritual knowing begins to unfold.

But what was the difference between humans and all these things in nature?

The tree fulfilled its mission; it did exactly what it was supposed to do. It changed carbon dioxide to oxygen. It had no trouble being a tree, doing what it needed to do.

Alex looked at his companions walking around the Petrified Forest. Each of the women were on their own part of the timeline, trying to figure out who they were. He looked at Cora and knew one of her lessons had to do with self-esteem— if I buy this, I'll feel better. If I have a big fancy house with all the fancy accoutrements, people will look up to me.

For Keri, her lesson had to do with self-love—if I'm loved, I'll feel better, never quite understanding that until she loved herself first, she would never find a satisfying love outside herself.

They were each at the point in their timelines where they were still gathering energy from each other, from physical things. They hadn't quite learned the lesson that the energies they craved were always there for them to tap into. It didn't come from people or things.

Glancing over at Zoey, he knew she still struggled with judgment. She still had a tendency to hold people to her own moral standards. Yet she was at a point in her spiritual journey where she was starting to let go of expectations for people. She was learning that she had to be okay with where they were in life. Each had their own path to follow, just as she did. At least she was aware of what she was doing and was starting to catch herself and correct her energy and thoughts.

It was a struggle, even for Alex, with all his knowings and experiences. Yet, he could never go backwards. He would never go back to the way his life was before he'd started on this journey. It was impossible. Each new knowing gave him more insight into why he experienced what he experienced. This trip was a perfect example of that. The whole thought process of the timeline and its geometric figures were opportunities to have an energetic experience to teach them who they truly were. And wasn't that what humanity craved for? To understand who they truly were and why they were created in the first place?

Alex noticed how each of his companions had a different energetic frequency according to what they were experiencing in the Petrified Forest.

Zoey's frequency was higher because she'd reached the stage of spiritual understanding that allowed her to look deeply into the experience of the moment. Her questions were always, what does this mean to me? How can I connect and unite with the energy of the experience?

Cora and Keri's frequency was lower because they were still at the stage of not quite seeing the energetic experience. Their thoughts were wrapped up in how hot the day was, or how much their feet hurt from walking. Alex didn't judge them. He found himself in a place where he loved them for the fact that they were on their timeline and were here having an experience.

To his amazement, he watched as Cora and Keri's energies and a geometric figure they each had in their energy field started to come together.

"Zoey, come here!" he exclaimed.

Zoey came running over. "What's going on?"

"Look at Cora and Keri. Do you see anything?"

Zoey squinted her eyes and studied them for a moment. "Not really. What am I supposed to see?"

"Focus on them for a minute. Be completely mindful. Get in their space, but don't judge them. Don't look at them as our friends. Just see them as human beings traveling on their timeline. Open yourself up as much as you can."

As Alex instructed Zoey what to do, he too opened up his senses. He heard Zoey gasp next to him and knew she was seeing what he was seeing—the geometric figures in their aura. Yet there was one geometric figure that stood apart from the others. This one was orange in color. He remembered his dream of the staircase and he instantly knew this was the geometric figure that held the lessons of emotion.

Alex and Zoey watched as Cora and Keri's vibrations started to rise. Their energies were attempting to match the color of the geometry. Suddenly, the two women shuddered as the vibration and the geometry collided, sending those tiny sparks of light cascading through them.

"Their geometric figures exploded!" Zoey gasped. She turned to stare at him in amazement. "Why? What just happened?"

Alex just smiled. "It's time to go," he said.

THE SEEDS *of* OUR EXPERIENCES

As it is with everything in nature, there is a seed that starts the process of growing. With humans, that seed is the sperm to the egg. We start so many things with our intentions. We plant seeds with our thoughts and deeds. Yet the energy of our intention is only as strong as where we are on our timeline.

Nature's geometry is perfect. As we've stated many times, nature is happy being nature. Humans, however, are driven to understand who and what we are. Along our timelines are the seeds, the opportunities to learn spiritual truths, to align with those geometric figures that hold the lessons we need to learn in order to move along and experience bigger and more wondrous things. Each geometric figure holds the next seed—the beginnings of a new lesson that, when learned, help us grow fully into who and what we truly are.

The Awakening

DESPITE ZOEY'S PRODDING, he wouldn't say anything more. She knew enough not to push him. Once he processed it within his own mind, he would share.

They finished their sightseeing and headed back to their hotel. On the way, while Cora and Keri chatted in the back seat, Zoey kept a sharp eye on Alex. She'd become sharply attuned to shifts of energy over the years and knew instantly when Alex's vibration started to dip down.

"Your energy just changed," she whispered to him. "What's going on?"

Alex chuckled. "You're a good friend. Thanks for paying attention and catching me. I've been thinking about what happened at the Petrified Forest. I think I understand it, but I still worry if I'm getting it right."

Zoey reached out and rested her hand on his arm. "If there's one thing you've always taught me, it's to surrender and wait and watch for the next thing to happen. So far the Universe or," she chuckled, "our timeline hasn't let us down. I'm sure the answer will come to you." She grinned at him. "Don't suddenly become like everybody else out there and try to control everything."

"Heaven forbid!"

Arriving at the hotel, they took off to their rooms to freshen up. The decision was made to meet back at Alex's room to decide where to go for dinner.

"Where's Keri?" Alex asked, as Cora and Zoey arrived at his room.

"She said she forgot something and ran back to her room to get it. She should be here any minute," Cora responded.

A few moments later, Keri knocked on the door and entered. "Sorry I'm late. I don't know why, but I had a feeling I should bring this." She winked at Alex. "I'm doing what you always tell me to do. When I get a knowing, I should follow my gut."

She dug into her pocket and pulled out a piece of petrified wood. Placing it on the nightstand, she laughed when she saw the look of horror on Alex's face. "Don't worry, I didn't steal it. All those signs warning not to take any of the petrified wood was enough to give me nightmares. I bought that at the crystal shop we went to."

Alex glanced over to Zoey and they shared a smile. Yes, even going to that crystal shop and experiencing all its energies served a purpose.

Keri stepped back. As she did so, she felt a strange sensation in her heart. In fact, they all felt it.

"What is that I'm feeling?" she asked as she unconsciously placed her hand over her heart.

"It's a vibration within your heart," Alex explained. "Your energy is going up and your heart is opening to higher truths."

"Wow. It's like getting a big, warm, safe hug in my heart."

"Is this a higher truth of love?" Cora asked as she too felt the warm sensation in her chest.

"Yes. Humans love things, love people, love food, but those are just aspects of love. This is a much higher experience of vibration."

"Is that piece of petrified wood really doing this to us?"

"The wood is serving as a reminder. Let's open up to this."

The four friends felt each of their hearts pulled along by the other's heart. Their combined vibrations continued to rise.

"Look around you," Alex instructed. "What do you see?"

Keri and Cora gasped as they saw bright bands of light swirling around their companions. "Oh my goodness! I'm seeing colors around you and Zoey!"

"What else do you see?"

Both ladies squinted their eyes. To their amazement, they began to discern geometric figures floating in Zoey and Alex's energy field.

"Those figures you've been talking about! They're...they're real!"

"Yes they are. I believe these geometric figures are trying to pull us towards the next geometric figure."

"What does that mean?"

"Think of the geometric figures as a seed. Your vibration is trying to get to the level where a switch is turned on for the seed to sprout."

"What happens when that switch is turned on?"

"Something wonderful."

Keri sucked in her breath as she felt herself expand. For a moment, she felt one with everything—with her friends, with the trees outside, with the birds, with the entire planet. "I can feel it. My heart is going deeper. I'm feeling all there is around me. It's absolutely divine!"

Keri and Cora had never felt anything like this before. They were seeing things they'd never expected to see. However, because they still had many lessons to learn on their timeline, their vibration couldn't quite reach to the level of the next geometric figure. The energy leveled off and began to sink. But they were left with a tingling of energy reverberating throughout their bodies.

They both sank down on Alex's bed, their faces bathed in amazement and awe.

"I don't know what just happened, but there are no words to describe how incredible that felt," Cora said.

"For a moment, you were able to feel that love that we humans all crave to feel," Alex explained. "The cool thing is that you felt it, not from a stone, or a thing, or even a person. You felt it from something higher and bigger than yourself. The reason you were able to feel that is because you learned a valuable lesson back at the Petrified Forest today."

"We did?"

"Do you remember shuddering just before we left?" Cora and Keri nodded. "I had the same experience sitting next to that petrified trunk."

"What was that?" Zoey asked.

"Each geometric figure holds the next lesson to be learned on the timeline. But what happens when the lesson is learned?" The women shrugged. "I believe that when your vibration gets high enough because you've learned the lesson, it joins with the geometric figure that holds the energy of that particular lesson and releases."

"Wow! So that was what I saw back at the Petrified Forest!" Zoey exclaimed. She turned to Cora and Keri. "When you felt that shudder back there, I actually saw a geometric figure in each of your energy fields explode and release energy into you."

Alex nodded. "The lesson you learned was that, despite all the crystals you bought in that store in an effort to own the energy, you've just discovered you are the energy. You surrendered to the moment and learned you didn't need that piece of petrified wood to do it. The energy you felt didn't come from that. It served as a reminder and brought you to a truth of who you are."

Keri reached over and picked up the piece of petrified wood. When she'd first bought it, she'd felt a tingle in her palm. Now there was nothing. There didn't need to be. Alex was right. She no longer needed a reminder of the energy. She *was* the energy.

"These figures are like a seed, the next unfolding, the next step in your spiritual evolutionary journey," Alex continued. "It represents the next experience, the next gift. Humanity has so much potential within it. As empaths, our quest is to continue to learn our lessons and what are truly the higher aspects of this vibration of love. We need to go higher and higher in this truth and allow the light to shine through us, surrendering to the moments the lessons each moment offers and learn them. Anything that keeps you stuck in your life keeps you stuck on your timeline. You need to have courage and trust and faith to walk into anything that grabs your attention and opens your heart. These experiences are put there for a reason. They're there to constantly remind you of who you are. The trees, the animals—they're perfect on their timeline. That's why we feel the love we do from them. Think of infants. Think of the love you feel when you hold a baby in your arms. At that moment, they're perfect with who they are. Unfortunately, babies lose that because of the demands of adults who place their fears and emotions on to them. So many children are born empathic, but instead of seeing it as the gift it is, they're overwhelmed by the world's drama and fears and unfulfilled energies thrown at them every day."

"Goodness," Cora replied. "That's a lot to think about. I think you're on to something."

Alex smiled. "Nope. I'm just on my timeline."

Cora and Keri were too overwhelmed by their experience to even think about eating. Zoey offered to sit with them to help them process the energies they'd felt. Alex decided to take a short walk outside to clear his head.

Walking out behind the hotel, he noticed a large hill. He felt a pull to climb it and as dusk fell, Alex made his way to the top. There, he found a large stone and sat down. He looked out over the surrounding desert, breathing in deeply of the cooling night air.

It was obvious he wasn't the first person to sit on this hill. He felt the energies of all the tourists who had make this short trek before him. Yet, through his empathy, he felt an underlying vibration, a tingle in his feet that told him the earth was trying to get his attention. He focused his mind on this vibration and noticed how the earth energy was rooting him to the space of this moment.

Is it possible, he wondered, that the earth is always trying to remind us physically of who we are at all times? He thought back over his life—to all those moments when he could have said no. When he could have rejected what he was feeling because of fear. Or ego. When he could have spent his days protecting himself and hiding away from all that he felt. Yet someway, somehow, he'd always found the courage to keep going. To go into the next experience. He'd reached a point in his life where he'd gotten sick and tired of always being sick and tired and decided there had to be something else out there. There had to be a method to the madness that was his life. And not just his life, but the lives of so many other empaths around him. Surely, there were others who had come before him who had started to understand the geometric figures—maybe even see them—but for whatever reason hadn't quite gotten as far on their timeline as he had. Maybe it just came down to energetic courage or a curiosity or a need to figure his life out.

The sun began to set over the desert, turning the sky into a spectacular panorama of reds and oranges. Sitting up on the rock, Alex felt a connection to all things, not just from now, but from the past. He felt a deep love for the peoples who had once inhabited these lands. For all the peoples since who were, like him, just trying to figure things out.

He felt a shift in his energy field and for the first time, he felt the hearts of others beyond the horizon who were grasping these spiritual truths. There were others out there who understood this, who saw the geometric figures, who felt the energies of the timeline. It gladdened Alex. He wasn't alone. He wasn't special. He was walking in the footsteps of other teachers, other seekers who had gotten sick and tired of being sick and tired and knew there had to be a reason for all they were going through.

He turned his thoughts back to how far he himself had come on his personal journey. So many lessons he'd gotten through—learning not to fear, learning how vibration works, learning energy dynamics. He realized, once again, how much of a gift his empathy actually was. No matter how fearful or painful or overwhelming his life sometimes was, there was always a way to get to the next level. Always something to learn that would help him navigate those difficult times.

It suddenly dawned on him that each time he'd learned the energetic lesson the moment was presenting, he would shudder. Now he knew what it was. It was the sacred geometry in his life telling him he'd accomplished what he was supposed to accomplish; he'd learned the lesson he was supposed to learn. The energy would then release and the next thing he knew, a new friend or a new opportunity would come into his life to get him to the next phase. To the next geometry that contained the next lesson to learn. It was just like that stairway he'd seen in his dream. Each step represented a lesson. As soon as he learned it, he'd climb to the next step and learn that lesson and so on until he reached the top where the gold temple was. Maybe that temple was the ascension everyone was always talking about. You had to earn that ascension step by step. And once you reached the temple, you were done. Like the petrified tree, your timeline was done. Your destiny was fulfilled.

Alex thought back to the people he'd met throughout his life. So many clamored to be who they thought they should be and what they thought their truth should be. Like the man on the plane. He'd worked hard to be what he thought he should be. But he wasn't happy. He became stuck on his timeline and his energy grew stagnant. He couldn't see that everything around him, around everyone, is always trying to remind us to get to the next energy, to the next geometry of our next truth. Because by doing that, it brings us to who we were really meant to be.

And just who are we supposed to be? Alex mused. The answer swiftly came to him. We who understand this and "get" it are the examples to others. We show that it can be done. It's not an easy journey by any means, but the rewards are worth it. To feel this love that words can't describe, to see the look of understanding on another person's face, to help them along the path you yourself have already trod upon—this is who and what we are meant to be. We become in service to others, just like the many teachers who have come before us.

Alex chuckled to himself. No one was going to want to hear this. They were all caught up with being who they think they should be. All those years he craved and worked towards becoming a rock star. Getting so close so many times. Only it never reached its logical conclusion. The same with Zoey and her desire to become a writer of fiction. Yet each learned valuable lessons from the experience. Instead of being bitter or continuing to knock their head against the wall or fighting tooth and nail to achieve what they think they wanted, they learned the lesson of simply being present no matter what. They didn't fall into the false belief that their lives were a failure. On the contrary. They found another path, another way to be. Their timeline allowed them to make a choice at that moment. They chose not to remain stuck in what at the time seemed to be an unfulfilled dream, but which instead led them to something bigger, something better, using the skills they'd learned along the way. They reached a point where they could truly say they were at peace with who they were. They achieved a calmness and peace of mind many others consider out of reach or impossible to attain.

They'd learned to surrender to be what they were supposed to be all along.

Alex sat up abruptly as a realization hit him.

Oh my God! That's the answer! In the dream I had with that man on the wall, he was constantly asking me when is it ever enough? When do people get to a point when it's enough? This is it! When you make peace with the process, it becomes enough. You understand there's a process unfolding and you become excited about what is coming up around the corner. You see that you're on a timeline to the next geometry that's going to change your life. Your responsibility is to understand that and to understand how your energy works. To see what you're getting and not getting and adjust your energy to that. Our life is a set of lessons to teach us about surrendering as to why we were created and what we are becoming. It's really that simple.

So many people leak their energy in judgment or fear or worry. So many people spend their lives protecting themselves from what they feel, not realizing that what they're doing is creating a wall and a container around themselves that is hard to move out of. They become mired in becoming a victim to the moment instead of seeing each energetic experience as an opportunity to learn from it.

So many people take energy from each other and never move forward because when they take energy from another person, their vibration is only as high as the vibration of the energy they're taking. The energy they crave is all around them. All they need to do is acknowledge it and reach out for it.

As Alex pondered these truths, he heard the sound of clapping behind him. Thinking a hotel guest had unexpectedly come up behind him, he turned and was surprised to find the luminescent man from his dreams smiling down at him.

"You've finally figured it out, haven't you?"

Alex nodded. "I have. The empath's quest is to find out when we finally have enough. Making peace with the process is the answer. It's what makes our life enough. It helps us trust that there really is a process to our lives. It isn't haphazard. We each have a timeline that adjusts as we move forward according to our choices. When the right energetic choice is realized, the geometry of the seed sprouts, acknowledging and creating our next set of choices. There's an excitement to that. To wondering and looking forward to what's next. And as we move along the timeline, it brings us that much closer to the golden temple I dreamed about. To reaching ascension." He paused, then offered the man a wide grin. "I don't suppose you can give me a clue as to what is next?"

The man shook his head, his eyes twinkling. "You'll see."

And with that, he disappeared.

Epilogue

THANK YOU for taking this journey with Alex, Zoey, Cora, and Keri. We hope the information in this book will help bring you to a calmer state of mind as you realize you do hold the power within your own hands to navigate your own life and your own timeline. As you proceed and learn the lessons life has to offer and you climb your own staircase towards ascension, you too will become the example to others. You will help them, and they in turn will help others and so on and so on. The community manifestation becomes a place where like-minded people come together, not to destroy, but to build and reach a place where you are truly at peace with yourself and the world around you.

It doesn't get any better than that.

We now have a website, www.comerfordwilson.com where you can drop by, ask questions, see what we're up to. We're on Twitter, and Facebook. We have also created a Facebook and Twitter page called Alex Empath, where we share quotes that you can contemplate as you go about your daily activities.

About the Authors

Bety Comerford and **Steve Wilson** are ordained Spiritualist Ministers, shamanic healers, psychics, and teachers with more than thirty years experience helping people to understand their empathic gifts, assisting those who wish to remove obstacles that keep them from living a more fulfilling life, and bringing an understanding of how the world works so everyone can successfully navigate their lives. Their first book, *The Reluctant Empath*, began teaching the quest. This book delves deeper.